Collins

Scottish
Wild
Flowers

SHETLAND
(c 60 miles N.E.
of Orkney)

ORKNEY

CAITH-NESS

LEWIS

HARRIS

SUTHERLAND

OUTER HEBRIDES

ROSS AND
CROMARTY

MORAY FIRTH

S. UIST

SKYE

Inverness

NAIRN

MORAY-SHIRE

BANFFSHIRE

ABERDEEN-SHIRE

Aberdeen

1

INVERNESS-SHIRE

PERTH-SHIRE

ANGUS

Dundee

MULL

ARGYLL

Perth

FIRTH OF TAY

FIFE

ISLAY

2 Stirling

4   5

3

FIRTH OF FORTH

6   Glasgow

Edinburgh

EAST LOTHIAN

8 BERWICK-SHIRE

LANARK-SHIRE

9

FIRTH OF CLYDE

BRAN

Ayr

AYRSHIRE

10 ROXBURGH-SHIRE

DUMFRIES-SHIRE

KIRKCUD-BRIGHT-SHIRE

Dumfries

WIGTOWN-SHIRE

SOLWAY FIRTH

Carlisle

1. KINCARDINESHIRE
2. DUNBARTONSHIRE
3. STIRLINGSHIRE
4. CLACKMANNANSHIRE
5. KINROSS-SHIRE
6. RENFREWSHIRE
7. WEST LOTHIAN
8. MIDLOTHIAN
9. PEEBLES-SHIRE
10. SELKIRKSHIRE

Collins

Scottish Wild Flowers

MICHAEL SCOTT

Michael Scott is a writer and broadcaster with a training in
botany and education, and a special interest in Scottish
mountain flowers. He has run many adult education classes on
wild flowers and leads natural history courses and study tours.
He is Scottish Officer of the conservation charity Plantlife and
edits *Scottish Environment News*.

For JGR and SS, two great companions on the hill.

HarperCollins*Publishers*
Westerhill Road, Bishopbriggs, Glasgow G64 2QT

First published 1995
This edition published 2000

10 9 8 7 6 5 4 3

ISBN 0 00 719736-5

Illustrations from *Collins New Generation Guide to the Wild Flowers
of Britain and Northern Europe*
Additional artwork by Valerie Price and Sue Scott
Photographs by the author unless otherwise stated

Also available in this series: *Collins Scottish Birds*

Printed and Bound by Printing Express Ltd., Hong Kong.

CONTENTS

INTRODUCTION

Whin or Gorse colours the landscape of many Scottish hillsides and sea-cliffs in summer

Scotland and its Flowers

A recent survey showed that scenery was one of the main attractions for 82 per cent of visitors to Scotland. Integral to that scenery are the wild flowers that colour the landscape: the purple of Heather on Highland hillsides in late summer, the occasional splash of red Poppies in lowland fields or the rich yellows of Gorse on a clifftop, for example.

This book is intended for visitors to Scotland and

residents who would like to know more about the flowers they see on their travels. It is designed to help identify the more conspicuous flowers likely to be met whilst exploring the scenic splendours of Scotland.

Scope of the Book

To include all 1,000 or so distinctive species of flowering plants in Scotland in a book this size would be impossible without extreme abbreviation. This book therefore concentrates on commoner species likely to catch the eye of anyone with a non-specialist interest in the Scottish flora. But because too much selectivity can be as frustrating as too much detail, brief comparisons are given in many cases between the plants covered and similar rarer species.

Grasses and sedges are excluded, despite their ecological importance, because they take practice to identify. Trees are also excluded, and coverage of superficially similar plants, such as Chickweeds and Dandelion-like flowers, has been reduced, since these too can frustrate the uninitiated.

Flowers likely to be seen only by intrepid hillwalkers are also omitted, although there are descriptions of commoner montane species which might be met beside a high-level road or in the relatively arctic environment of the far north-west. Most importantly, the book ignores southern plants which are rare in Scotland, but includes introduced species which have become a conspicuous part of the Scottish landscape.

The aim is to help readers appreciate the attractions and complexities of the Scottish flora. Hopefully, this will, in time, encourage the identification of more 'difficult' plants, using some of the excellent comprehensive flower guides now available.

How to use the Book

Unfortunately, there is no shortcut to wild flower identification. However, by basing this book around the habitats in which plants grow, it is possible to reduce the options for any flower encountered. Thus, in a sand-dune, wood or peat bog, for example, only relatively few plants are likely to occur, and most of these should

Heather is very much part of the Highland landscape, turning glorious purple in late summer.

be identifiable with a few moments leafing through the relevant pages in this book. Key features to confirm identification are highlighted in *italics* in the species accounts. Not all plants are restricted to one habitat, but, where relevant, a cross-reference is made at the beginning of a section to other habitats sharing similar species, and these, and the rest of each chapter, should be checked if the section for a particular habitat does not yield immediate identification.

Each chapter opens with an essay on the habitats covered. Most of the species mentioned are described in detail later in the chapter or elsewhere in the book, although a few not featured elsewhere are indicated by including their scientific names.

Habitats are arranged from those most influenced by humans, progressively towards wilder and more remote areas. Within each habitat, species are arranged roughly in the traditional scientific order. This is based on floral structure, so that, generally, simple flowers with a whorl of obvious petals are considered first, and those described later are progressively more specialised in form.

A Brief Guide to Terminology

For ease of use, most technical terminology has been avoided, even where this leads to slight simplification. However, it is impossible to describe a flower without naming its parts, as illustrated in the Creeping Buttercup (below). It is helpful to consider the flower as a series of concentric rings of 'leaves' which become progressively more specialised towards the centre. Thus, the outer **sepals**, which protect the flower in bud, are generally like a leaf in shape and colour. The ring of **petals** inside them retain a leaf-like shape, but are

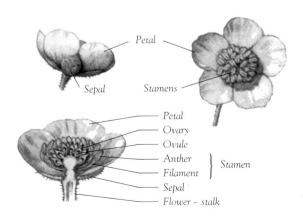

usually brightly coloured to attract pollinating insects and allow the flower to set seed. Plants whose pollen is dispersed by the wind therefore need only small, inconspicuous petals. In some flowers, the sepals and/or petals are united into a **tube**, while other plants have all their flower-lobes either sepal-like or petal-like.

The ring of club-shaped **stamens** within the petals carry pollen (male sex-cells) in a swollen capsule called the **anther**. The innermost 'leaves' form one or more **ovaries**, enclosing the **ovules** or female sex-cells. The ovary is topped by a pollen-receptor, the **stigma**, which is often held on a stalk called the **style**.

After fertilisation, the ovules develop into **seeds** and the ovary swells to form a **fruit**. This need not be fleshy like the fruits in a greengrocer's shop, but can be any shape from the 'pepper-pot' of a Poppy fruit, to a pouch-like **capsule** or a **pod** like a pea-pod.

Beneath the **inflorescence** (the branching or clustered grouping of flowers), some plants have a further set of leaves called **bracts**. These may or may not be the same shape as other stem leaves.

Other unavoidable technical terminology is the distinction between **shrubs**, which have at least some wood in their stems, and **herbs** which lack woody stems. Finally three terms are used to describe different plant lifecycles: **annuals** flower briefly then set seed and die, with only their seeds surviving to germinate and grow in the next flowering season; **biennials** germinate and develop in their first season, but do not flower until the second year, after which they die; and **perennials** can survive through several growing seasons, although not necessarily flowering in each. A few other terms relevant to particular groups or families are introduced as they occur in the guide.

Naming Names

The naming of flowers is another potential source of confusion. Whilst some plant names are in everyday use, less common or conspicuous species often lack popular names. Furthermore, common names can vary even around a small country like Britain. Thus, for example, the 'Bluebell of Scotland' is known as Harebell in England, and the plant known as Bluebell in England is called Wild Hyacinth in Scotland. In a bid to reduce ambiguity, the Botanical Society of the British Isles (BSBI) has produced a recommended list of names (*English Names of Wild Flowers*; Dony, Rob and Perring, 1981) and the style of these names has generally been followed, except where Scots names are in wide usage, in which case the 'official' English name is included in the text. However the excessive punctuation of some recommended names has been avoided, so the widely-used name Cranesbill has been preferred, for example, to the contrived Crane's-bill.

The system of scientific nomenclature is designed to avoid such confusion and produce an international standard. Unfortunately, scientific names are in a state of flux as they are amended in the light of changing scientific understanding of plant relationships and as older names (which have priority by the rules of nomenclature) are unearthed. The scientific names used here follow the current standard British work (*New Flora of the British Isles*; Stace, 1991).

However, so that at least one cultural tradition is not lost, Gaelic names of plants are included for the first time in a popular work of this sort. Gaelic is the traditional language of the north-west Highlands and islands of Scotland. Usage can vary from area to area, and by no means every flower has a Gaelic name, but the names reproduced here are based on a list of recommended names compiled for the BSBI by Joan Clark and Ian MacDonald. The author is grateful to the society for permission to reproduce these names, and to the compilers for providing their literal meanings, where possible*. Some of the explanations have been abbreviated for space, and any resulting misinterpretation is the author's alone.

Description of Areas

The geographical range quoted for each species refers to Scotland only, and is based on interpretation of maps in the *Atlas of the British Flora* (Perring and Walters; 1962), augmented by reference to local floras.

For clarity, abbreviations have been avoided in these descriptions, other than the use of N, E, S, and W for directions. N Isles is used for Orkney and Shetland, W Isles for the Outer Hebrides, and W islands for all islands on the western seaboard of Scotland. Other areas are referred to by traditional county names, which are still widely used despite local government reorganisation in 1974 and 1996 (see map on p. 2).

Responsible conduct

Although not enshrined in law, there is a tradition of freedom of access on foot to all wild land in Scotland, but this relies on a responsible attitude by all involved. Please therefore respect the legitimate interests of the landowner, ensure that all gates are left as found, keep dogs on leads, and avoid disturbance and damage to stock and crops. In particular, access in Highland areas

---

*On some occasions Cameron (*Gaelic Names of Plants*, 1883) is quoted, although the compilers may not necessarily agree with his translation.

may be limited during the deer-stalking season, generally from early August until February; always check with the relevant estate if access is desired during this period.

Wild flowers can brighten the most unexpected corners of Scotland, like these Foxgloves and Yellow (Flag) Iris beside a Highland road.
Photo Sue Scott

A BOTANICAL CODE OF CONDUCT

- Do not dig up any wild plants.
- Always leave wild flowers for others to enjoy.
- To identify a flower, take this guide to the plant not *vice versa*.
- If a sample is essential to identify a plant, take the smallest adequate piece **only** if the plant is common.
- Take great care when studying or photographing one plant not to accidentally trample another.
- If a rare plant is discovered, avoid exposing it to unwelcome attention by making a path or flattening vegetation around it, and do not reveal its locality to anyone who will not respect that confidence.
- Always consider the needs of other wildlife and, in particular, avoid disturbance to breeding birds.

13

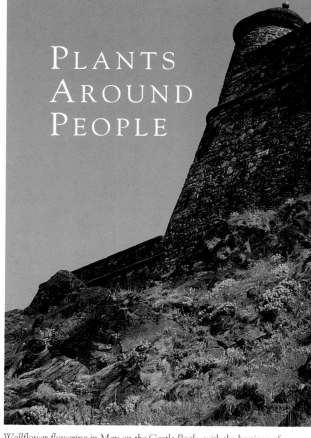

PLANTS AROUND PEOPLE

Wallflower flowering in May on the Castle Rock, with the bastions of Edinburgh Castle towering above

The plants that live closest to people in Scotland – in cities and wasteground, fields and roadsides – are the least markedly Scottish in this book. Plants have been carried so widely by human activities that most of these 'domesticated' plants will be familiar to anyone from mainland Europe and several even to American visitors.

Indeed, many of the most conspicuous flowers of wasteground in Scottish cities are not native here.

14

For example, the Butterfly-bush, which can colonise the most inhospitable city gap sites, is a native of China which escaped from gardens early this century. Similarly, Wallflower, which blooms abundantly over Edinburgh Castle Rock in May and perches on several other Scottish castles, originated in the western Mediterranean.

Perhaps the most remarkable story is that of Oxford Ragwort, now one of the commonest plants on untended walls, cracked pavements and wasteground in Edinburgh and Glasgow. A native of Sicily and southern Italy, it was brought to the botanic garden in Oxford in the 18th century. By 1794, it had escaped onto walls nearby, and from there it began to spread slowly. The clinker of railway lines provided a perfect habitat, and trains helped carry its parachuted seeds. It reached Edinburgh around 1948, Dundee by 1967 and as far north as Shetland in 1986.

Oxford Ragwort and Rosebay Willowherb growing in an urban gap site

15

Where Oxford Ragwort meets up with Groundsel, an all-too-abundant garden weed, the two hybridise. The resulting cross – which looks like groundsel but with stubby, yellow, petal-like rays – is infertile, and so cannot spread. However, in Leith in Edinburgh, a chance twist of its genetics produced a fertile plant, which is true-breeding in its own right and so a 'proper' species. Because this 'new' plant was found first (quite independently) on a roadside in Wales, it is called Welsh Ragwort (*Senecio cambrensis*).

A dense stand of Rosebay Willowherb

Not every city plant is an introduction from exotic parts. Rosebay Willowherb is perhaps the most abundant plant of disturbed ground in Scottish cities. It is native, but 80 years ago it was only found in damp woods and rocky places. The burnt-out bomb sites of the Second World War provided exactly the right sort of damp, nitrate-rich soil for it to establish, and – with each plant producing 80,000 seeds which float in the wind like a snowstorm – it soon spread more widely.

Outside cities, any drive around Scotland in spring or summer is enlivened by the roadside flowers. Many roadside verges are linear, left-over fragments of wild vegetation that once flourished in the area – woodland or heathland for example. Lime-loving plants such as Cowslip, Crosswort and Bloody Cranesbill add colour to some coastal roads in east Scotland, while quiet verges in the far north-west can provide a display of orchids to rival any garden.

Roadside members of the carrot family may seem off-putting to all but the most dedicated botanist, but the delicate fern-like foliage and frothy heads of Sweet Cicely are always a delight, even if a name cannot be put to the plant. It was probably introduced as a pot-herb, and has been taken as far north as Orkney and Shetland.

Increasingly, wildflower seed is being planted into the verges of new roads to soften their impact on the landscape. Seeds of Red or White Clover are often sown in newly-laid soil because of the enriching effects of their nitrogen-fixing roots. Other wild flowers are

A handsome plant of Sweet Cicely on a roadside verge in Perthshire

17

included for their beauty and in recognition of the value of verges as wildflower refuges. Some species appear of their own accord. The seeds of Common Poppy, for

It is rare today to see such a massed display of Corn Marigold, a victim of herbicides and cleaner seed corn

example, can live in the soil for 20 years, ready to spring up after road-building machinery has passed.

Beyond the verges, arable fields seem bare in comparison. Herbicides and cleaner seed-corn have eliminated the colourful (but troublesome) displays of wild flowers that once graced field margins. Occasionally, a field may miss its spring spraying, and a glorious sheet of red poppies or yellow Corn Marigold may briefly brighten the countryside, although nowadays a field of yellow is more likely to be cultivated Rape. The increasing proportion of land 'set aside' from agriculture as a result of European Union policy is also adding more variety to fields, although often only thistles and docks benefit.

Even grassland and meadows are often devoid of colour as a result of intensive agricultural methods and heavy grazing by sheep and deer. Only resilient and adaptable species like buttercups and thistles grow in many over-used pastures, while Daisy, Yarrow and Sheep's Sorrel are the only flowers to brighten many heavily-grazed hillsides in the Southern Uplands. A precious few 'left-over' meadows, several of which are now protected as nature reserves, remain to remind us of former glories. In north-west Scotland, however, traditional, low-intensity pastoral agriculture still survives, supported by the uniquely Scottish system of crofting in which a part-time farmer has heritable and legally-protected tenant's rights to a small-holding. Here, rather more of the traditional field-edge plants are left to flower.

The best displays are found on the exposed western seaboard of the Outer Hebrides and Sutherland. The prevailing winds here carry white shell-sand from the beaches inland to cover the underlying peat. This produces a thin soil which the crofters fertilise with seaweed and plough shallowly to grow barley or potatoes, with long periods left fallow. The result is the *machair*, the flat, fertile fringe of the crofting lands which still supports a colourful abundance of flowers in summer.

A rich display of colourful weeds around a crofter's potato field in South Uist are a reminder of fields before the advent of herbicides

Wallflower

Erysimum cheiri
CABBAGE FAMILY

Varieties of this familiar garden plant from Greece with *bright yellow flowers* have been established since medieval times on castle walls (see p. 14) and old stonework, scattered through the Borders, E and SW. Typically of the cabbage family (p. 45), it has *4 petals*, but no wild relative has *such large and showy flowers* with *petals up to 2 cm long*. It stands up to 60 cm tall, with crowded, *hairy, narrowly-oblong leaves*, violet-scented spring flowers and *long, cylindrical seedpods*.
Gael: Lus Leth an t-Samhraidh ('Half of Summer Plant')

Procumbent Pearlwort

Sagina procumbens
PINK FAMILY

Because this *mat-forming perennial* can resist trampling and likes nutrient-rich soils, it grows abundantly in paths, lawns, roadside verges, arable fields and wet, stony ground all round Scotland. Its *rooting branches, with moss-like leaves, creep along the ground*. Its flowers, in summer, are tiny with 4 (*rarely 5*) green sepals and *petals which are either minute and white or totally absent*.
Gael: Mungan Làir ('Creeping Mungan' = ? bully or ? after St. Mungo)

OTHER SPECIES: Two other petal-less pearlworts are upright growing annuals: Sea Pearlwort (*S. maritima*), with *blunt-ended leaves*, grows on coastal dunes and cliffs, and Annual Pearlwort (*S. apetala*), with *leaves tapering to a long point*, is uncommon in bare ground in the S and E. (See also Knotted Pearlwort; p. 104)

20

Rosebay Willowherb

Chamerion angustifolium
WILLOWHERB FAMILY

This handsome perennial originally inhabited damp woods and rocky places, but woodland clearance and wartime bombing encouraged its spread into wasteground and urban gap sites throughout Scotland (see p. 16), although less commonly in the NW, W Isles and Shetland. Its creeping roots produce *dense patches of slightly hairy stems*, 1 m or more tall, with numerous, *spirally-arranged, narrow, lance-shaped leaves*. In mid- to late-summer, it has *dense spikes of deep-pink, 4-petalled flowers*, with the *upper 2 petals broader than the lower 2*. The flowers develop into *long, thin fruit capsules, which split into 4*, releasing a snowdrift of white seeds.

Gael: Seileachan Frangach ('French Willowherb')

Butterfly-bush

Buddleja davidii
BUDDLEIA FAMILY

Another plant of urban gap sites, Buddleia (as it is often known) was introduced from China last century and has escaped from gardens at scattered sites around Scotland, including only Mull and Islay amongst the islands. A shrub to 5 m tall, it has *toothed, narrowly egg-shaped leaves* that are *white-felted beneath*. In summer and early autumn, it produces *dense, pyramidal heads of lilac or purple flowers*, with an *orange ring at the mouth* of a cylindrical petal-tube. The pollen-rich flowers are much visited by butterflies.

Gael: Preas an Dealain-dè ('Butterfly's Bush')

Ivy-leaved Toadflax

Cymbalaria muralis
FIGWORT FAMILY

This attractive plant is instantly recognisable on sunny old walls by its *rather fleshy, often purplish ivy-shaped leaves* and *lilac and yellow snapdragon-like flowers* in spring and summer. Its delicate *purple stems* trail over the wall, and root in the mortar. It also occasionally colonises lime-rich rocks. Introduced from Italy and the Alps, it was first recorded in Britain in 1640, but is now widespread in S and C Scotland, especially in towns. It is more scattered in the NE and along the W coast, and generally absent from the Isles.

Gael: Buabh-lion Eidheannach ('Ivy Toadflax')

Oxford Ragwort

Senecio squalidus
DAISY FAMILY

An alien with an unusual history (p.15), Oxford Ragwort is now a common plant of old walls, wasteground, railway tracks and even cracked pavements in sunny spots in Edinburgh and Glasgow, flowering from late spring to autumn. It is less common elsewhere in Scotland, but is still spreading northwards. It is distinguished from the more widespread Common Ragwort (p. 59) by its bushier growth, shorter, hairless *stems, not exceeding 30 cm tall*, and *more open, spreading inflorescence*. The *outer bracts* clasping the base of each daisy-like flowerhead are *black-tipped*, and the flowerhead usually has *13 yellow, petal-like rays*.

Gael: Buaghallan Pheadair ('Peter's Ragwort' (see p.59))

Groundsel

Senecio vulgaris
DAISY FAMILY

Vulgaris means common, and Groundsel lives up to this scientific name, flowering abundantly all year round in wasteground, arable fields and gardens throughout Scotland, being sparser only in the C Highlands. Its *yellow button heads* normally lack the spreading ray florets of other ragworts, and have *black-tipped bracts* as in Oxford Ragwort (occasional plants with short, stubby ray-florets may be a hybrid between these 2 species). The *densely-clustered buds* and *mostly hairless leaves* are also characteristic.

Gael: Grunnasg ('Ground One')

A single groundsel can produce 1,000 seeds and have 3 generations in a year, making it an aggressive colonist of gardens.

Daisy

Bellis perennis
DAISY FAMILY

Daisy grows in short grassland and disturbed ground throughout Scotland, flowering abundantly from early spring to late autumn. Its rosette of *glossy, spoon-shaped leaves* hug the ground, escaping both grazing animals and lawn-mowers. As in all its family, its 'flowers' – on hairy, leafless stalks – are a cluster of tiny florets (see p.60). The showy, outer ray-florets are *white, often tinged with pink*, and the central, fertile florets form a *yellow disc*.

Gael: Neòinean ('Noon-flower')

The name 'daisy' comes from 'day's eye', recording how the ray-florets spread open by day and close up at night.

Welsh Poppy

Meconopsis cambrica
POPPY FAMILY

A *hairless, yellow-flowered* poppy, native to Wales and SW England (as well as Spain and France), Welsh Poppy is widely grown in gardens. It occasionally escapes and is found at scattered sites near houses, usually sheltered by a wall or bank, in the Borders and Lowlands, and less commonly in the N and Isles. Its *leaves* are *divided into toothed, pointed, oval lobes*. It flowers in early summer, and develops into an *egg-shaped fruiting capsule* which characteristically splits into *short teeth at the tip*, unlike true poppies (p. 44) which shed their seeds through a pepper-pot of pores.

Gael: *Crom-lus Cuimreach* ('Welsh Poppy': *crom-lus* = 'bent plant')

Garlic Mustard

Alliaria petiolata
CABBAGE FAMILY

This handsome, late-spring flower is so familiar on roadsides, hedgerows and woodland edges in England that it earns the affectionate nickname 'Jack-by-the-Hedge'. It is less common in Scotland, and absent from most of the NW and Isles. Its rather *glossy and crisped, pale-green, heart-shaped leaves smell strongly of garlic* when crushed. Its basal leaves are long-stalked and stem leaves shorter stalked. Its stems, up to 1 m or more in height, are topped by a cluster of *white, 4-petalled flowers*, about 6 mm across, which develop into a *long, narrow, up-curved fruit pod*.

Gael: *Gàirleach-callaid* ('Hedge Garlic')

Red Campion

Silene dioica
PINK FAMILY

In early summer, the *deep pink flowers* of Red Campion enliven hedgerows and wood margins over most of Scotland, except the far NW. It also grows on mountain rock-ledges and seacliffs where seabirds enrich the soil. Its rather *robust, hairy,* sometimes rather sticky *stems* stand to 90 cm tall, with *oval to oblong leaves,* the upper of which are *short-stalked.* The clustered, tubular flowers are about 2 cm across, with *hairy, rather swollen sepal-tubes,* and spreading *petal-lobes* which are *deeply notched at the tip.*

Gael: Cìrean Coilich ('Cock's Comb')

N Isles plants (p. 245) have deeper red flowers and very hairy stems.

White Campion

Silene latifolia ssp. alba
PINK FAMILY

Similar in size and shape to Red Campion, this species is more restricted to the Lowlands and E, with few sites in the W. Probably an ancient introduction, it grows in wasteground, fields, roadsides and grassy banks. It can be distinguished by a *glandular-hairy stem, white, evening-scented flowers* in summer, and a swollen *fruiting capsule* with 10 *erect teeth* at the tip (down-turned in Red Campion).

Gael: Coirean Bàn ('Little White Cauldron')

When Red and White Campion meet, they hybridise freely. Because the hybrids are fertile, much interbreeding takes place and pink-flowered hybrids are commoner in many areas than either parent.

CRANESBILLS

The familiar cranesbills (*Geranium* species) of waysides, woods and meadows have leaves that are roundish in outline but often deeply and intricately cut. Their showy flowers are pinkish, purplish or bluish, with 5, often notched petals and 10 conspicuous stamens. The characteristic fruiting pod (right) is long and beaked (like the bill of a crane – *geranos* in Greek), and, when ripe, its outer walls rip away explosively from the central stalk, catapulting the seeds out.

Wood Cranesbill

Geranium sylvaticum
CRANESBILL FAMILY

Widespread in upland meadows, hedgebanks and woods in the Borders and C Highlands, Wood Cranesbill stands about 50 cm tall, with *hairy stems* and *reddish-mauve flowers* up to 3 cm in diameter ripening to *erect-growing fruits*. Its long-stalked *leaves* usually have 7 lobes, which are *toothed or shallowly cut around their margins*. It flowers, abundantly in places, from June to July, and is also a showy component of the 'tall-herb community' of mountain rock ledges.

Gael: Crobh Preachain Coille ('Crow's/Raven's Claw of the Wood')

OTHER SPECIES: The more lowland Meadow Cranesbill (G. *pratense*), with *violet-blue*, rather *larger flowers* (to 4 cm in diameter), more *deeply-cut leaves*, and *fruits which hang downwards* in pairs when young, and become upright as they mature, is found in meadows and roadsides in S and E Scotland, and occasionally elsewhere, including on the Isles, as a garden outcast.

Dovesfoot Cranesbill

Geranium molle
CRANESBILL FAMILY

This low-growing annual has *densely hairy stems* and *rounded, softly hairy, 5- to 9-lobed leaves*. Its small pink *flowers*, which grow in pairs on longish stalks in spring and summer, are *less than 1 cm across*, with *deeply-notched, rosy-purple petals* and *hairy sepals*. It grows in dry grassland, including sand-dunes, cultivated land and waste places all round Scotland, but is uncommon in the C and NW Highlands.

Gael: *Crobh Preachain Mìn* ('Soft Crow's/Raven's Claw')

OTHER SPECIES: The similar Small-flowered Cranesbill (*G. pusillum*) is much less common in cultivated and waste ground in E Scotland. It is *more robust*, with *smaller, deeply lobed, dull-lilac flowers* (less than 6 mm across) and *hairy fruit capsules*.

Herb-Robert

Geranium robertianum
CRANESBILL FAMILY

A straggly, summer-flowered annual of open woodland, hedgebanks, rocks and shingle, Herb-Robert has rather fragile, *reddish stems* and *deeply-lobed leaves* with only *scattered hairs*. Its *flowers* are often paired, *up to 2 cm across*, and have rather narrow, *wedge-shaped* pink *petals*, *rounded and not notched* at the tip, and *orange or purple anthers*. It is found around Scotland, although much more locally in the N, rare in the W Isles and probably introduced in N Isles.

Gael: *Lus an Ròis* ('Plant of the Rose') or *Ruideal* (possibly 'Red-haired')

27

Common Mallow

Malva sylvestris
MALLOW FAMILY

This robust perennial grows to 90 cm in height, with a *sparsely hairy stem*, and *roundish, gently lobed leaves*. The clustered *pinkish-purple flowers*, which appear in mid- to late-summer, are up to 4 cm across, with *purple-veined petals, which are deeply notched at the tip*. It grows on roadsides and waste places in SE Scotland and the Moray Firth area, with a few scattered W coast sites.

Gael: Lus nam Meall Mòra ('Plant of the Big Clusters')

OTHER SPECIES: Musk Mallow (*M. moschata*) with *deeply-cut*, narrow-lobed *stem leaves* and *rosy-pink or white flowers*, 3-6 cm across, is found much more rarely in E Scotland.

Bramble

Rubus fruticosus agg.
ROSE FAMILY

Specialists recognise around 300 'microspecies' of this common wayside plant, varying in growth form, shape of the leaves and prickles, size and colour of petals, and even the taste of the fruits. To the generalist, the *arching, prickly stems* with *toothed, 3-lobed leaves*, the 5-petalled white or pink flowers, 2-3 cm across, and the *glossy black, raspberry-like fruits* (technically a cluster of 1-seeded 'drupelets') are familiar enough in bushy places, woods and roadsides throughout most of Scotland, although scattered in the Highlands and W Isles, rare in Orkney and absent from Shetland.

Gael: Dris (plant); Smeur (berry) (perhaps from Smior = marrow)

Dog Rose

Rosa canina
ROSE FAMILY

This is the commonest of several wild roses inhabiting woods, hedges and scrubland around most of Scotland, including the Isles. They are bushy shrubs with *prickly, arching stems*, often 3 m or more long, and leaves with *1-3 paired leaflets* topped by a single leaflet. Their pink or white flowers are 3-5 cm across, with 5, often *notched*, petals. These ripen into *rose hips*, formed from the fleshy base of the flower, which swells to enclose the true fruits (the 'pips' inside).

Gael: Ròs nan Con (as English)

OTHER SPECIES: *R. caesia*, with downy or hairless leaves, is commoner in parts of the Highlands. Downy-roses (*R. tomentosa*, *R. sherardii* and *R. mollis*), with downy leaves, are also widespread. They are best separated on the form of their hips.

Broad-leaved Willowherb

Epilobiu n montanum
WILLOWHERB FAMILY

Willowherbs (see p. 162) have *4 rose-coloured petal-lobes* on top of a *long flower tube*, which extends after fertilisation into a *narrow, cylindrical fruiting capsule*. This is the commonest Scottish species, found in hedgerows, woods, rocks and gardens throughout Scotland except for parts of the Highlands. It is distinguished by its *hairless, broadly egg-shaped, stalked leaves* and by the *cross-shaped stigma* (see flower detail).

Gael: Seileachan Coitcheann ('Common Willowherb')

CARROT FAMILY

Members of this family (called umbellifers) are typically tallish, white- or yellow-flowered plants of bushy or grassy places, with much-divided, often lacy or fern-like, leaves. Characteristically, their tiny flowers are clustered on stalks, which spread out like the spokes of an umbrella into convex or flat heads. This apparent uniformity can confuse beginners, but, with practice, species can be distinguished by leaf shape, stem form and the presence of bracts and bracteoles (see diagram). The best identification feature is the shape of the fruits, when present. *The Scots name 'Kecks' is used for the plant and dry, hollow stems of several umbellifers, but most typically of Hogweed.*

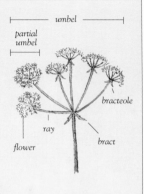

Sweet Cicely

Myrrhis odorata
CARROT FAMILY

Of the 3 commonest roadside umbellifers (see also opposite), Sweet Cicely is the first to flower abundantly, producing glorious displays in roadsides (see p. 17), woods and grassy places in S and E Scotland from May to June. It stands to 1 m or more tall, with *downy, fern-like leaves*, which are *white-blotched* at their centres when young and *smell of aniseed* when crushed. Its *densely-crowded flowerheads* are slightly creamy. The *narrow, flask-shaped fruits* have *prominent ridges covered in bristles*. Introduced for culinary use, it is commonest in populous areas, absent from hilly districts, and only grows near houses in the N Isles.

Gael: Mirr (from the Biblical name)

30

Cow Parsley

Anthriscus sylvestris
CARROT FAMILY

Although it flowers from April, Cow Parsley becomes the dominant roadside umbellifer as Sweet Cicely fades in June. It is distinguished by its *hollow, furrowed stem*, to 1 m tall and *hairy at the base*, and its *more finely-divided leaves*. Its *inflorescence is more widely-spaced*, and *lacks bracts* (although with 4-6 bracteoles beneath each umbel). Its *flowers* are *3-4 mm across*, ripening into *smooth, blackish, narrowly egg-shaped fruits*. It grows in hedgerows and bushy places over most of Scotland, but rarely in the NW.

Gael: *Costag Fhiadhain* ('Wild Little Aromatic One')

OTHER SPECIES: Bur Chervil (*A. caucalis*), with *flowers 2 mm across, hairless stems* and *fruits with hooked spines*, is rare in E Scotland.

Hogweed

Heracleum sphondylium
CARROT FAMILY

The last of the 3 common roadside umbellifers to flower, in July to September, Hogweed grows in grassy places, woods and hedgerows all over Scotland, but sparsely in the N. It is taller (to 2m), with coarser, rough *leaves*, which are *once-divided* into broad, toothed lobes and *sheath the hollow stem* at their base. Its *inflorescence* is *flat-topped* and pinkish, and its clustered *fruits*, up to 8 mm long, are *round, flattened and pale*. (cf Giant Hogweed, p. 168).

Gael: *Odharan* ('Dun-coloured One')

Rough Chervil

Chaerophyllum temulum
CARROT FAMILY

Superficially similar to Cow Parsley (p.31), although shorter, Rough Chervil flowers slightly later (in June and July). It is distinguished by its *rough, purple-spotted stem, covered with short, stiff hairs* and *swollen at the joints*. Its delicately-cut *leaves* are *softly hairy*. The inflorescence has an irregular, diffuse shape and usually lacks bracts. The *fruit* is *flask-shaped, narrowing towards the tip*, 6 mm long, and often purplish. Rough Chervil is restricted to hedgerows and grassland in E Scotland and the Morayshire coast, with a few sites in the SW.

Gael: Costag Ghiobach ('Hairy Little Aromatic One')

Upright Hedge-Parsley

Torilis japonica
CARROT FAMILY

Another hedgerow and grassland umbellifer, this flowers just after the previous species in July and August. It is never as conspicuous in roadside verges as the trio on the previous pages, being generally shorter and less bushy in growth. Its *stem* is covered in *down-turned bristles* and feels *rough when rubbed upwards*. Its *flowers* are *pinkish or purplish-white*, and it has *small, spiny, egg-shaped fruits*. It is widespread in S and E Scotland, occasional in the W Isles and absent from NW Scotland and the N Isles.

Gael: Peirsill Fàil ('Roadside/Verge Parsley')

Ground-Elder

Aegopodium podagraria
CARROT FAMILY

Sometimes called Bishop's Weed, this all-too-troublesome perennial, familiar to gardeners, spreads by *far-reaching underground stems* which break when dug and form new plants. Its elder-like *leaves* have 3 lobes, themselves often divided into 3 and toothed round the edge. Its *stems* are 40-100 cm tall, *hollow and grooved*. Its dense, white inflorescence *lacks bracts and bracteoles*, and develops into *egg-shaped fruits*, which are *ridged and 3-4 mm long*. The plant has been spread into cultivated land widely across Scotland, including the Isles, but not in parts of the C and N Highlands.
Gael: Lus an Easbaig ('Bishop's Plant')

Wild Angelica

Angelica sylvestris
CARROT FAMILY

An impressively robust plant to 2 m tall, Wild Angelica has a *hollow, purplish stem*. Its large, rather rough *leaves* are *neatly divided into narrow egg-shaped lobes* and the base of the leaf-stalk swells into an inflated sheath around the stem. The *inflorescence* is neatly rounded with *hairy stalks* and *no bracts*, and the *egg-shaped fruits are flattened with broad, marginal wings*. It grows in damp meadows, roadside verges, woods, marshes and mountain cliff-ledges in all parts of Scotland, although sturdy Shetland plants may be escaped Garden Angelica (*Angelica archangelica*).
Gael: Lus nam Buadh ('Plant of the Virtues')

DOCK FAMILY

Known as dockens in Scotland, members of this family are not at first easy to separate, largely because their wind-pollinated flowers are so reduced. The best distinguishing features are the shape of the leaves and the inner 'sepals', which enlarge into hard valves around the 3-sided fruits and often bear prominent warts. All dockens have undivided leaves, borne singly and narrowing up the stem. Their small, greenish flowers are densely clustered into spikes which top the stems in summer and early autumn, and become more crowded as the reddish fruits develop. Several are persistent farmland and garden weeds. The Gaelic for Docken, *Copag*, means 'Little Tufted One'.

Curled Dock

Rumex crispus
DOCK FAMILY

The tallest and most ubiquitous docken, Curled Dock is found in waste places, cultivated land and pastures throughout Scotland, including the Isles, except for some parts of the Central and NW Highlands. It stands 30-100 cm tall, with *wavy-edged, pointed, lance-shaped leaves* to 25 cm long. It has rather *leafy flowering spikes*. Its *heart-shaped fruit valves* are *toothless* and 1, 2 or all 3 of them have a *smooth, oblong wart*. It can also survive wet conditions in pond margins, saltmarshes and coastal shingle.

Gael: Copag Chamagach (as English)

34

Broad-leaved Dock

Rumex obtusifolius
DOCK FAMILY

Broad-leaved Dock has a similar distribution to Curled Dock but is the commonest docken of roadsides. It is less abundant in pastures, preferring open habitats such as field margins, ditches and waste ground. It has *broader, more egg-shaped, blunt-tipped leaves*, to 15 cm across, which are often *heart-shaped at the base*. Its triangular fruit valves are *strongly-toothed with a round wart*.

Gael: *Copag Leathann ('Broad Dock')*

The leaves of this docken are rubbed on the skin to soothe the stings of nettles, with which it commonly grows.

Clustered Dock

Rumex conglomeratus
DOCK FAMILY

A slighter species, rarely exceeding 50 cm in height, Clustered Dock has slender, wavy stems with *widely-spreading branches* and *narrowly oval leaves*. Its flowers and fruits are borne in *knot-like clusters* on branches which are *leafy almost to their tip*. Its oval *fruit valves* have *large, swollen warts*. It grows mainly in marshy meadows, ditches and stream-sides in C and E Scotland.

Gael: *Copag Bhagaideach (as English)*

OTHER SPECIES: Northern Dock (*R. longifolius*), which replaces Curled Dock in parts of the E Highlands, lacks warts on its fruit valves. Wood Dock (*R. sanguineus*) has more narrowly-angled branches and a small wart on 1 fruit valve only; it grows in woodland, roadsides and wasteground. See also Monk's Rhubarb (p. 170).

Japanese Knotweed

Fallopia japonica
DOCK FAMILY

The Victorians introduced this handsome but aggressive plant into their gardens from Japan about 1825, and it soon escaped into the wild. Today, it is widespread in the C Lowlands and Moray Firth area, and more localised throughout the rest of Scotland, including the Isles. It forms dense thickets along the upper shores of some west coast sea-lochs.

Its *wavy, reddish stems* die back each year but grow rapidly in the spring to *2 m tall*. Its *oval leaves* are *drawn out into a long tip* and *sharply cut-off at the base*, and its *dingy-white flowers* appear in short tassels between the leaves in late summer and early autumn.
Gael: Glùineach Sheapanach (from the English)

Giant Knotweed

Fallopia sachalinensis
DOCK FAMILY

Introduced to Britain by 1861, Giant Knotweed is even taller than Japanese Knotweed (*up to 3m*) and it was therefore grown in fewer gardens. As a result, it is much less widespread in the wild, with just a few, scattered, mainly coastal sites, including on the W Isles. Its *leaves* are *longer* (15-30 cm, compared to 6-12 cm), *pointed but less drawn-out at the tip* and often *heart-shaped* at the base. Its *greenish flowers* appear in shorter, denser inflorescences in late summer.
Gael: Glùineach Shagailìneach (from the English)

Bittersweet

Solanum dulcamara
NIGHTSHADE FAMILY

Also known as Woody Nightshade, this shrubby plant is found only in the lowland areas of S Scotland and around the Moray Firth. Its weak, downy stems scramble through hedgerows and scrub in woods and waste ground, reaching 2 m or more in length. It has *oval leaves*, often with *2 lobes at the base*, and distinctive *flowers* with a *yellow central column* and *5 purple petal-lobes which bend backwards* as the flowers mature. These develop into mildly poisonous *berries* which are green at first, and ripen through yellow *to red*.

Gael: Fuath Gorm ('Blue Aversion' or 'Blue Hate')

Common Toadflax

Linaria vulgaris
FIGWORT FAMILY

Although nowhere frequent, the showy flowerheads of Common Toadflax brighten some roadsides, wasteground and grassland around the lowlands and E Scotland from mid-summer to autumn. The plant stands 30-80 cm tall, and spreads by creeping runners, sometimes forming dense patches. It has *narrow, lance-shaped, greyish leaves* and long spikes of *snapdragon-like yellow flowers*, with a *3-lobed lower lip and an orange 'mouth'*. Only bees are heavy enough to open this mouth and have sufficiently long tongues to reach nectar stored at the base of the long spur beneath the flower.

Gael: Buabh-lion Coitcheann (as English)

Foxglove

Digitalis purpurea
FIGWORT FAMILY

This familiar flower grows commonly in woods, heaths and rocky places throughout Scotland, although it is only a rare garden outcast in Shetland. It is particularly abundant in woodland clearings and burnt moors. It is biennial, producing *downy, wrinkled, tongue-shaped leaves* in its first year and a 50-150 cm tall flowering stem in its second summer, with 20-80 *thimble-like flowers which are deep pink outside and creamy with purple spots inside*. White-flowered plants occur occasionally, but large numbers may suggest garden origin.
Gael: Lus nam Ban-sìdh ('Fairy Women's Plant')

Hedge Woundwort

Stachys sylvatica
THYME FAMILY

Hedge Woundwort is most easily recognised by its *pungent odour when crushed*. It stands up to 1 m tall, with *roughly hairy, coarsely-toothed, heart-shaped leaves* and a spike of *claret-red, 2-lipped flowers, about 15 mm long*, with pale blotches on the lower lip. It is common in woods and hedgebanks over most of Scotland, but rare in the W Isles and absent from Shetland (where a similar-looking hybrid with Marsh Woundwort (p. 176) occurs as a garden escape).
Gael: Lus nan Sgor ('Plant of the Notches/Sharp Rocks')

OTHER SPECIES: Field Woundwort (*S. arvensis*), a paler- and smaller-flowered annual, grows in scattered arable fields, mostly in coastal areas.

Red Dead-nettle

Lamium purpureum
THYME FAMILY

This annual of cultivated and waste ground is found throughout Scotland, although more rarely in the Highlands and NW. Its sprawling, much-branched, *square stems* are 10-45 cm tall, and its *pungent, nettle-like but non-stinging leaves* are stalked and hairy *with rounded marginal teeth*. Typically of its family, it has tubular, 2-lipped *flowers*. These are *pinkish-purple*, 10-15 mm long, and appear from spring to autumn, tucked among purple-tinged bracts. The flowers have a long petal-tube *projecting beyond the cup of the sepals*, with a ring of hairs near the base of the petal-tube.

Gael: Caoch-dheanntag Dhearg (as English; caoch = 'blind/empty'))

White Dead-nettle

Lamium album
THYME FAMILY

Taller-growing than the previous species (to 60 cm tall) and *perennial*, White Dead-nettle spreads by creeping, underground runners to form *dense patches* in places. Its *creamy-white flowers* are *rather larger* than those of Red Dead-nettle (20-25 mm long), with a *hooded upper lip* and also with a ring of hairs near the base of the petal-tube. It flowers from early summer well into winter, in hedgebanks, roadsides and wasteground in the lowlands and the E of Scotland only.

Gael: Teanga Mhìn ('Smooth Tongue')

If the petal-tube of a fresh flower is carefully removed, sweet nectar can be safely sucked from its base.

Hedge Bedstraw

Galium mollugo
BEDSTRAW FAMILY

Bedstraws typically have whorls of 4 or more narrow leaves around square stems, and clusters of small tubular flowers with 4 joined petals. Hedge Bedstraw fits this pattern, with *weak, scrambling, much-branched stems, lacking hairs or prickles*. Its stem is *markedly swollen beneath each whorl of 6-8 oblong leaves*, which are 8-30 mm long, with *forward-pointed marginal prickles*. The stem is topped by *widely-branched clusters of white flowers*, rarely more than 4 mm across. Hedge Bedstraw is uncommon in hedgebanks, grasslands, scrub and wasteground in S and E Scotland.

Gael: Màdar Fàil ('Madder of the Hedge')

Cleavers

Galium aparine
BEDSTRAW FAMILY

Cleavers is also known as Goosegrass or Sticky Willie in Scotland. The abundance of names reflects the familiarity of a plant which is found abundantly across Scotland in hedges and wasteground, as well as coastal shingle and lime-rich mountain screes. Its *stems are weak and scrambling*, breaking readily, and like its leaves and peppercorn-sized *fruits, are covered in hooked bristles*. These allow the fruits or portions of stem to be transported in animal hair or human clothing, so spreading the plant. Its *flowers are pale green and no more than 2 mm across*, almost lost amongst the green bracts.

Gael: Garbh-lus ('Rough Plant')

Lesser Burdock

Arctium minus
DAISY FAMILY

The common name summarises this plant, which has downy, *dock-like leaves* and *oval, bur-like fruits*, about 2 cm in diameter, covered in *hooked bristles* which spread the fruits in fur and clothing. It is a sturdy biennial to 1 m or more in height, with many arching stems, and *egg-shaped, purple thistle-like flowerheads*. It grows in open woodland, roadsides and waste grounds, although rarer inland in N Scotland and the Isles.

Gael: Leadan Liosda (perhaps 'Stiff Locks' (of hair))

Common Knapweed

Centaurea nigra
DAISY FAMILY

Also known as Hardheads, this thistle-like plant of grassland and waysides is best recognised by its tight heads of purple florets. These are borne on an oval cup, *2-4 cm in diameter*, of *dark brown bracts*, which are cut into long, fine teeth at their tips. The rigid stems can be 60 cm tall and the leaves are often gently lobed. The plant grows throughout Scotland, although less commonly in the N.

Gael: Cnapan Dubh ('Little Black Knob')
Children use the hard heads and stems like conkers in the game of 'sojers' (soldiers).

OTHER SPECIES: Greater Knapweed (*C. scabiosa*), with *deeply-lobed leaves* and *larger flowerheads* usually with *showy outer florets*, grows around the E coast and in N Sutherland.

BUTTERCUPS

Most buttercups (*Ranunculus* species) are perennials with leaves that are deeply cut into toothed lobes and often hairy. The flowers typically have 5 golden-yellow, overlapping petals (a) and 3-5 green sepals (b), ripening into a tight cluster of single-seeded, egg-shaped fruits held in a roundish head (c). They flower in spring to summer.

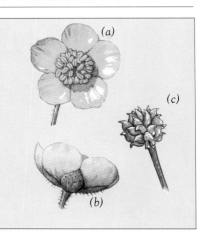

Meadow Buttercup

Ranunculus acris
BUTTERCUP FAMILY

The commonest buttercup throughout Scotland, including the Isles, Meadow Buttercup is found in damp meadows and pastures on all but the most acid soils. It also grows in roadside verges, damp ditches, open woodland and mountain rock-ledges, and varies in height from 15-100 cm, depending on soil conditions. Its flowers are 15-25 mm across, with 5 green *sepals held upright against the flower*. Its *flower-stalks* are *unfurrowed* and *covered with hairs*, which are *flattened against the stalk*. The *softly-hairy leaves* are divided into 3-7 narrow, wedge-shaped lobes, but are *roundish in outline*.
Gael: *Buidheag an t-Samhraidh* ('Little Yellow One of Summer')

Like many of its family, Meadow Buttercup is avoided by grazing animals, because it is highly acrid and very poisonous; this allows it to flourish at the expense of other species in heavily-grazed pastures.

Creeping Buttercup

Ranunculus repens
BUTTERCUP FAMILY

Although slightly less widespread than Meadow Buttercup, Creeping Buttercup can be even more abundant in heavy, nutrient-rich soils. It grows in wet pastures and woods, ditch-sides, and damp sand-dune hollows. It spreads by *creeping, surface runners* which *root at intervals* and form new plants when trampled by livestock. Its *flowers* are *rather larger* (20-30 mm in diameter), on *furrowed, hairy stalks*, usually with 5 or 6 (but up to 9 or more) petals and *upright or spreading sepals* (see box opposite). Its leaves are more *triangular in outline*.
Gael: Buidheag ('Little Yellow One')

Bulbous Buttercup

Ranunculus bulbosus
BUTTERCUP FAMILY

The least common of the 3 field buttercups, Bulbous Buttercup grows scattered throughout the lowlands, particularly near coasts. It prefers drier and more lime-rich pastures, including sand-dunes and W Isles machair, but is intolerant of trampling. It is distinguished by its *furrowed, hairy flower-stalks, down-turned sepals*, leaves with a *long-stalked middle lobe*, and *swollen, bulbous stem base*.

Gael: Fuile-thalmhainn (perhaps 'Blood of the Earth')

OTHER SPECIES: Two annual buttercups grow found uncommonly in fields in S Scotland. Hairy Buttercup (*R. sardous*) has *down-turned sepals* but no bulbous stem base. Corn Buttercup (*R. arvensis*) has *small flowers* (to 12 mm across) and *spiny fruits*.

Common Poppy

Papaver rhoeas
POPPY FAMILY

This attractive annual is widespread in disturbed ground and waste places in SE Scotland, but rarer in the N and W. Herbicides have reduced its abundance, although it is coming back in set-aside farmland. Its showy *flowers*, in June to September, are *5-10 cm across* with *4 scarlet petals* which are often *dark-blotched* at the base. Its pepperpot-like *seed capsule* is *roundish to egg-shaped*.

Gael: Meilbheag (perhaps 'Little Pestle' from meil = grind)

OTHER SPECIES: Long-headed Poppy (*P. dubium*) grows further north than Common Poppy, including the W Isles machair. Its *flowers are 3-7 cm across, pale scarlet* and usually *unblotched*, ripening into a *smooth, club-shaped fruiting capsule*. Prickly Poppy (*P. argemone*), with *smaller flowers, pale scarlet petals* and *long capsules covered in prickly hairs*, is found scattered along the E coast and around the Clyde.

Common Fumitory

Fumaria officinalis
FUMITORY FAMILY

This is the commonest of several, very similar fumitories which are easily overlooked in field margins on light soils. They have *delicate, feathery greyish-green leaves* and spike-like heads of about 20 *tubular pink flowers*, 7-8 mm long, *tipped with deeper crimson*. Common Fumitory is most frequent in E Scotland, less common in the SW and scattered in the Isles.

Gael: Lus Deathach-thalmhainn ('Earth-smoke Plant')

CABBAGE FAMILY

Members of this family, like Turnip (right) are called crucifers from the characteristic cross shape of their flowers, which typically have 4 free (ie. not united) petals, 4 sepals and 4 or 6 stamens. They ripen into capsule-like fruits which are variously cylindrical or oval in shape and split from the base to disperse the seeds. Crucifer leaves are usually lobed or toothed, and leaf and capsule shape, together with flower colour, are the main identification characters. The abundant seeds and opportunistic annual growth of crucifers means that many are weeds of disturbed ground.

Rape

Brassica napus
CABBAGE FAMILY

Almost 60,000 hectares of rape was grown in Scotland in 1993. Because its beaked, *cylindrical fruits* need to be mature before oil can be extracted, some seeds inevitably are shed, and rape is rapidly becoming established as the commonest yellow crucifer in roadsides and wasteground around the lowlands. It flowers from May until August, with *pale-yellow flowers* which sit *below the developing buds*. Its *leaves* are *bluey-green*.

Gael: Raib (from the English)

OTHER SPECIES: Wild Turnip (*B. rapa*), with *deeper-yellow flowers* whose stalks expand so that the flowers *overtop the buds* (see box above), and *grass-green lower leaves*, grows in roadsides and wasteground in lowland arable areas.

Charlock

Sinapis arvensis
CABBAGE FAMILY

An annual plant of heavy soils, Charlock grows in arable fields and disturbed ground throughout agricultural Scotland, including the Isles. Its much-branched *stems* are covered in *coarse, down-turned hairs*. Its *leaves* are spear-shaped and often purplish, the *lower ones stalked and partly lobed at the base*, and the *upper ones stalkless*. It flowers in early summer, with 4 bright-yellow petals, and *sepals* that *spread outwards*. The bristly *fruiting pod* is tipped by a *straight beak, about half as long as the seeded portion*.

Gael: Sgeallan (perhaps 'Kernel')

Although this troublesome weed is easily controlled by herbicides, its seeds can remain viable in the soil for 50 years.

White Mustard

Sinapis alba
CABBAGE FAMILY

The mustard of mustard-and-cress, this annual from the Mediterranean region is grown as a forage crop and for green manure in cultivated lowland areas, and is sometimes accidentally introduced with grain or bird seed. It is found in scattered areas, mostly in E and NE Scotland. It resembles Charlock but has *stalked, irregularly but much-lobed leaves* and its hairy *pod* ends in a *flattened, curved beak, at least as long as the seeded portion*. Its seeds are mixed with those of Indian Mustard to make commercial mustard.

Gael: Sgeallan Bàn ('White Sgeallan' - see above)

Winter-cress

Barbarea vulgaris
CABBAGE FAMILY

The *large, oval terminal lobe* of the much-divided, glossy-green leaves distinguish this species from all other yellow-flowered crucifers. Its small flowers appear in spring and summer, with their *sepals held tightly against, and about half as long as, the petals*. The cylindrical *fruit pod* retains the *short style at its tip*, and is *flattened or 4-angled*. Winter-cress is a biennial or perennial of fields, waste ground, riverbanks and roadside verges around S and E Scotland.

Gael: Treabhach (may relate to treabh = 'plough')
Formerly grown for winter salads, winter-cress was harvested in December around the feast day of St Barbara, commemorated in its scientific name.

Hedge Mustard

Sisymbrium officinale
CABBAGE FAMILY

This annual or overwintering weed flowers in early summer in hedgebanks, fields, roadsides and wasteground throughout agricultural areas of Scotland, but is absent from the C and NW Highlands and Shetland. Its *stem*, which is often covered in down-turned bristles, stands stiffy erect, *with wiry branches almost at right-angles*. The *tiny flowers (about 3 mm across)*, which appear mainly in summer, have *pale-yellow petals*, and develop into long, rather hairy pods which are *pressed tightly against the stem*.

Gael: Meilise (derivation obscure)

47

Wild Radish

Raphanus raphinastrum
CABBAGE FAMILY

This annual of cultivated land, wasteground and roadsides is found throughout the lowlands, including the N Isles, but in the W it is commoner on islands than the mainland. Its *leaves* are deeply-lobed, with a *large end lobe* and *side lobes rapidly shrinking towards the leaf base*. Its typical crucifer, 4-petalled *flowers*, which appear in summer, resemble Charlock (p. 46), but are *yellow, white or lilac* and have *upright sepals*. The best distinguishing character is the cylindrical *pods*, which are up to 8 cm long, *constricted between each of the 3-8 seeds* and end in a *slender beak*.

Gael: Meacan Ruadh Fiadhain ('Wild Red Plant')

SUBSPECIES: Sea Radish (subspecies *maritimus*) is a taller plant with larger, yellow flowers, *more crowded leaf-lobes*, and *fewer, larger seeds* in its pods. It grows on cliffs, shingle and dunes on SW coasts.

Smith's Pepperwort

Lepidium heterophyllum
CABBAGE FAMILY

Another crucifer of cultivated places and waysides, this hairy perennial is restricted to S and E Scotland. Its *narrow, toothed leaves* cluster round and *clasp the stems*, which are topped in summer by *long, crowded heads* of *small, white flowers*. These develop into oval, 2-seeded *fruits* with *broad wings* and a *short style in a notch at the tip*.

Gael: Piobar an Duine Bhochd ('Poor Man's Pepper')

Shepherd's Purse

Capsella bursa-pastoris
CABBAGE FAMILY

This annual or biennial crucifer is found in cultivated land, paths, roadsides, wasteground and sand dunes in all but the most mountainous areas of Scotland. Its *leaves*, which form a *neat rosette* on the ground or *clasp the stem*, are *spear-shaped* in outline, but vary from deeply-toothed to almost undivided. The *tiny, white flowers, 2-3 mm in diameter*, are present throughout the year, and develop into *heart-shaped pods*, resembling a medieval shepherd's purse.
Gael: An Sporan ('The Purse')

Wavy Bitter-cress

Cardamine flexuosa
CABBAGE FAMILY

Related to Cuckooflower (p. 157), Wavy Bitter-cress has similar, *roundly-lobed leaves*, but much smaller flowers (about *4 mm across*), with *6 stamens*. It has rather zigzag, hairy stems, with *few leaves in a basal rosette* and *more stem leaves*. Its fruit pods are long and narrow. An annual to perennial summer-flowering crucifer, it grows in moist, shady places from mountain springs to woods, wasteground and gardens, through most of Scotland, but is a garden outcast in Shetland.
Gael: Searbh-bhiolair Chasta (as English)

OTHER SPECIES: The very similar Hairy Bitter-cress (*C. hirsuta*) has *more rosette-leaves, few stem-leaves*, and only *4 stamens*. It grows in rather drier ground, including gardens and greenhouses, throughout Scotland.

Field Pansy

Viola arvensis
VIOLET FAMILY

A typical pansy (p. 65), this is distinguished from the similar Wild Pansy (p. 65) by its smaller *flowers (no more than 20 mm vertically)* with *cream-coloured or violet-tinged petals*, which are *shorter than the pointed sepals*. As a final check, *the spur* behind its flower is *no longer than the backward-pointed flaps at the base of its sepals*. It flowers in spring and summer in cultivated and waste ground in E Scotland, the N Isles, and W coastal regions and islands.

Gael: Luibh Cridhe ('Heart Plant/Weed')

Common Mouse-ear

Cerastium fontanum
PINK FAMILY

This is the commonest of several similar annuals or short-lived perennials, also called Mouse-eared Chickweeds, widespread in cultivated ground and grassland around Scotland. All have weak, sprawling stems, *oval leaves with whitish hairs* (resembling mouse ears), *5 sepals not joined in a tube*, and *5 notched petals*. This species has particularly *deeply notched petals*, which are *just longer than the sepals*.

Gael: Cluas Luch Choitcheann (as English)

OTHER SPECIES: Field Mouse-ear (*C. arvense*), with narrower leaves and *petals twice as long as the sepals*, grows in dry grassland in E Scotland. Sticky Mouse-ear (*C. glomeratum*), with *white-hairy sepals equalling the petals in length*, is widespread in arable fields and open grassland.

Common Chickweed

Stellaria media
PINK FAMILY

This annual weed of cultivated ground, roadsides, waste places and even the upper shore of saltmarshes, is recognised by the *single line of hairs* down its straggly *stems* between each opposite pair of *egg-shaped, hairless leaves.* The lower of these leaves are long-stalked but the upper ones are stalkless. Its flowers are small, with *white petals a little shorter than the sepals* and 3-8 stamens with *purplish anthers.* It is common throughout Scotland, except for mountainous areas.

Gael: Fliodh (same word as that for 'Excrescence')

Thyme-leaved Sandwort

Arenaria serpyllifolia
PINK FAMILY

A low, slender, much-branched annual, this *greyish-green* sandwort grows in open ground, gardens and wall-tops, scattered over most of Scotland except for the NW and N Isles. Its *oval leaves* are *pointed at the tip* and, like its stems, are *covered in rough hairs.* It has a branched inflorescence of many small flowers (to 8 mm across) with *undivided white petals shorter than the pointed sepals,* and *flask-shaped fruits.*

Gael: Lus nan Naoi Alt Tiomach ('Thyme Plant of Nine Joints')

OTHER SPECIES: Spring Sandwort (*Minuartia verna*), a tufted perennial with *strongly 3-veined leaves* and *shining white flowers to 12 mm across,* grows in a few scattered base-rich rocky areas.

Corn Spurrey

Spergula arvensis
PINK FAMILY

An often troublesome annual weed of acid, sandy soil in fields, tracks, gardens and wasteground, Corn Spurrey is found in all but the Scottish uplands. It has *weak, straggling stems*, often covered in *sticky hairs*, and *narrow, fleshy, rather greyish leaves* in *whorl-like tufts* up the stems. Typically of its family, it has 5 sepals, showing between 5 rather narrow, undivided *petals, which·are white* and *slightly longer than the sepals*. It flowers in mid-summer, and the egg-shaped *fruit capsules* which then develop *hang sharply downwards* when young.

Gael: *Corran-lìn* ('Rough Flax') or *Cluain-lìn* (perhaps 'Fraudulent Flax')

Fat-Hen

Chenopodium album
GOOSEFOOT FAMILY

In the same family as Spinach and Beet, Fat-Hen is an annual with tiny flowers, in late summer, arranged in narrow spikes on *reddish stems* to 1.5 m tall. Its rather fleshy *leaves vary from spear- to egg-shaped* with at least the lower ones toothed, and often have a *white, mealy covering*. It grows in waste places and cultivated land, scattered through the lowland areas of Scotland.

Gael: *Càl Slapach* ('Slovenly Kale')

OTHER SPECIES: Good-King-Henry (*C. bonus-henricus*), a perennial, with *triangular, green leaves, pointed at the bottom corners* has escaped from cultivation to grow in nitrogen-rich soils near cultivation, mostly in the SE.

Sun Spurge

Euphorbia helioscopa
SPURGE FAMILY

The 'flowers' of Spurges consist of a cluster of tiny, petal-less flowers, enclosed within a greenish bract which has conspicuous lobes or glands. Sun Spurge is the most widespread Scottish species, found in cultivated, lowland areas, but declining with herbicide use and commonest now on W Isles machair. It has *blunt-ended, finely-toothed leaves*, which *taper to a narrow base*, and *round-lobed bracts*.

Gael: *Lus nam Foinneachan ('Plant of the Warts')*

OTHER SPECIES: Petty Spurge (*E. peplus*), found less commonly in fields and gardens, is *smaller and more branched* with *short-stalked, untoothed leaves* and *kidney-shaped bract lobes with slender horns*.

Common Nettle

Urtica dioica
NETTLE FAMILY

Virtually universal in Scotland, this perennial forms dense patches in hedgebanks, woods, grassy places, and disturbed ground, especially near buildings. Its egg-shaped leaves are coarsely-toothed with *stalks about half as long as the blade*. They are usually covered in *stinging hairs* which break when grasped, injecting formic acid. Tiny, wind-pollinated flowers hang in summer in tassels in the angles of the upper leaves.

Gael: *Deanntag or Feanntag (derivation obscure)*

OTHER SPECIES: Small Nettle (*U. urens*), an *annual* with *long-stalked leaves*, grows in cultivated and waste ground in E Scotland and the Isles.

Redshank

Persicaria maculosa
DOCK FAMILY

An abundant annual weed of arable fields, wasteground, waysides and marshy land, Redshank is absent only from mountainous areas. It has reddish, hairless stems to 75 cm tall but varying greatly in their degree of branching and uprightness. At the base of each lance-shaped, often *dark-blotched* leaf, the stem is swollen and encircled by a *membranous sheath topped with bristles*. The dense, stubby spikes of *pink flowers* appear in summer and early autumn.

Gael: Glùineach Dhearg ('Red Jointed One')

OTHER SPECIES: Pale Persicaria (*P. lapathifolia*), with *greenish flowers*, *unblotched leaves*, and *more truncated sheaths lacking bristles*, grows in similar habitats in scattered lowland areas.

Knotgrass

Polygonum aviculare
DOCK FAMILY

Another abundant annual of disturbed ground, arable fields and gardens, Knotgrass has a similar distribution to Redshank. It is much-branched, often spreading low over the ground, with *oval leaves* which are larger on the main stem than on the flowering branches. Small, *knot-like clusters of tiny pink or white flowers* grow in the angles of the leaves from summer to early winter.

Gael: Glùineach Bheag ('Small Jointed One')

OTHER SPECIES: Three similar, closely-related species are grouped as knotgrasses, one of which (*P. boreale*) is restricted to the far N and W.

Black Bindweed

Fallopia convolvulus
DOCK FAMILY

The *stalked, heart-shaped leaves* and *clockwise-twining stems* of this scrambling or climbing annual weed resemble those of the true Bindweeds (see p. 57), but the *flowers* are very different. They are *small and rather inconspicuous*, with 5 greenish-white petals, borne on stalks at the end of the stem in summer and autumn, and ripen into *dull black, triangular fruits*. The plant is a frequent weed of arable land, wasteground and gardens, mostly in E Scotland but is rare in the N and W including the islands.

Gael: Glùineach Dhubh ('Black Jointed One'; perhaps from glùn = 'knee')

Bugloss

Anchusa arvensis
BORAGE FAMILY

This *bristly-haired* annual grows in sandy or lime-rich fields, rarely far from the coast and probably spread by agricultural activities. It is fairly widespread in E Scotland, including the N Isles, rarer in the W mainland, but most common today in machair fields of the W Isles. It stands to 50 cm tall, with *narrow, wavy, tongue-shaped leaves*, the upper ones *half-clasping the stem*. Its flowers open in summer, with 5 spreading, *bright blue petal lobes*, united into a tube at their base. The *tube* is *abruptly kinked in the middle* and blocked by *conspicuous white scales* at its throat. (cf Green Alkanet, p. 141).

Gael: Lus Teanga an Daimh ('Ox-tongue Plant')

Field Forget-me-not

Myosotis arvensis
BORAGE FAMILY

Like many of their family, Forget-me-nots have blue flowers (often pink in bud) with a tubular base and spreading petal-lobes, arranged in inflorescences curled like scorpions' tails. This is the commonest dry-land species, standing to 60 cm tall with downy, lance-shaped leaves. It flowers in spring and summer in cultivated land, wasteground, roadsides, woods and sand-dunes throughout Scotland. It is an annual or biennial with *small flowers (less than 4 mm in diameter)*, borne on *stalks longer than the sepal-tubes*, which are covered in *hooked hairs*, and the style, tucked deep inside the flower, is shorter than the sepal-tube.

Gael: *Lus Midhe Aitich* ('*Midhe Plant of Cultivation*'; *Midhe obscure*)

Field Madder

Sherardia arvensis
BEDSTRAW FAMILY

This delicate, trailing annual is found in dry arable fields, open grassland and hedgebanks in the lowlands of E Scotland and near coasts in the W and N. It has whorls of 4-6, *oval, pointed, bristle-edged leaves* around a rather weak, squarish, often much-branched stem, which is *prickly at its angles* and 5-40 cm long. In summer and autumn the stems are tipped with small, clustered heads of 4-6 *pale-lilac flowers*, each with a slender tubular base, 4 spreading petal lobes, and 4-6 persistent teeth on the sepal-tube.

Gael: *Màdar na Machrach* ('*Machair Madder*')

Hedge Bindweed

Calystegia sepium
BINDWEED FAMILY

True bindweeds typically have twining stems that scramble over vegetation or fences, and showy, funnel-shaped flowers. This is the most widespread Scottish species, growing in hedges and bushy places around the lowlands, but nowhere commonly. Its weak stems, with large *heart-shaped leaves*, can scramble for over 3m. Its *flowers* are white or pinkish, about *3-4 cm across*, with *2 sepal-like bracts about 1.5 cm wide* under the flower, enclosing but *not hiding* the true sepals beneath.

Gael: *Dùil Mhial (derivation obscure)*

OTHER SPECIES: Large Bindweed (*C. silvatica*) is a rarer garden escape, mostly in the C lowlands. Its flowers are *around 6 cm across*, white or banded with pink, with *large, swollen bracts up to 3 cm wide, hiding the sepals*.

Field Bindweed

Convolvulus arvensis
BINDWEED FAMILY

Altogether a smaller plant, this is distinguished by its *arrow-shaped leaves* and *smaller flowers (2-3 cm across)*, which are often deeply suffused with pink and have only *tiny bracts*, well below the true sepals. It is a troublesome weed of cultivated land, wasteground and hedgebanks in the E and C lowlands, with underground stems which spiral down to depths of 2m and give rise to new plants if broken during cultivation.

Gael: *Iadh-lus ('Surrounding/Encompassing Plant')*

Henbit Dead-nettle

Lamium amplexicaule
THYME FAMILY

Henbit grows in low-intensity cultivated land in the E lowlands and W coasts. It has *rounded, wavy-edged leaves* (fancifully nibbled by hens), the *upper stalkless ones seeming to encircle the stem*. Its *pinkish-purple flowers*, in whorls up the stem, have a *narrow petal-tube, much longer than the sepals*, with a hooded upper lip and *strongly 2-lobed lower lip*.
Gael: Caoch-dheanntag Chearc ('Hen Dead-nettle'; caoch = blind/empty)

OTHER SPECIES: Northern Dead-nettle (*L. confertum*), with *stalkless upper leaves not encircling the stem* and *petal-tubes hardly longer than the sepals* grows in cultivated ground mostly in N coastal areas.

Common Hemp-nettle

Galeopsis tetrahit
THYME FAMILY

Although similar to Dead-nettles, Hemp-nettles have 2 small bumps near the base of their petal-tubes. This species is widespread in arable land and occasionally woods in all but mountainous areas. It is an annual with *roughly-hairy stems swollen beneath each pair of hairy, oval, toothed leaves*. The *white, pink or purple flowers* often have dark blotches on the *3-lobed lower lip*, and their *petal-tube is no longer than the sepals*.
Gael: Deanntag Lìn ('Flax Nettle')

OTHER SPECIES: Large-flowered Hemp-nettle (*G. speciosa*), with *pale yellow flowers with a violet lower lip*, grows in peaty lowland fields.

Common Ragwort

Senecio jacobaea
DAISY FAMILY

Although legally an 'injurious weed' which farmers must control because it is poisonous to grazing animals, Common Ragwort remains abundant in overgrazed pastures, wasteground, roadsides and sand-dunes throughout Scotland. A biennial or perennial to 1.5m tall, it has *finely-divided rosette leaves*, which wither before flowering, and similar leaves up the stem, which is crowned in summer and autumn by a *flat-topped inflorescence* of yellow daisy heads, *around 2 cm across*. The heads are enclosed by *bracts, the outer 2-5 of which are much shorter than the rest*. Some plants in N Scotland have button-like heads, lacking the showy outer 'ray florets'.(cf Oxford Ragwort, p. 22)

Gael: Buaghallan (possibly 'Victorious/Virtuous/Toad Plant')

Coltsfoot

Tussilago farfara
DAISY FAMILY

Flowering *from February* in some areas, Coltsfoot has *sturdy, scaly, purple stems*, topped by *solitary golden-yellow daisy heads*. These droop after flowering but return upright when the fruits are ripe to be carried off on tufts of silvery hair. After the flowers pass in April, *large, heart-shaped leaves* begin to develop, *edged with purple teeth* and *covered in a whitish down* that soon washes off the upper surface but is retained beneath. Coltsfoot is common in disturbed ground, tracks, dunes and screes throughout Scotland.

Gael: Cluas Liath ('Grey Ear')

59

DAISY FAMILY

Members of this family have tiny flowers, called florets, clustered into a head resembling a single large flower and surrounded by sepal-like bracts. In many species, such as Scentless Mayweed (right), the outer florets have their petal-tubes expanded on one side into showy petal-like 'rays' to attract pollinating insects. The inner 'disc' florets are purely reproductive. Some species have only disc or ray florets.

Scentless Mayweed

Tripleurospermum inodorum
DAISY FAMILY

The commonest daisy-like weed of cultivated and waste ground, Scentless Mayweed (illustrated above) is found throughout the lowlands and islands. It has typical daisy *flowerheads, to 4 cm across* with a *flat, yellow disc* and *white rays*. Its weak stem rarely exceeds 50 cm long, and its bushy *leaves* are divided into *fine hair-like segments* (cf Ox-eye Daisy, p. 91).

Gael: Buidheag an Arbhair ('Little Yellow One of the Corn')

OTHER SPECIES: Sea Mayweed (*T. maritimum*) (p. 102) of coastal cliffs and dunes has *fleshier leaves* and *stems spreading over the ground*.

Pineapple-weed

Matricaria discoidea
DAISY FAMILY

A successful introduction from Asia via North America, first recorded in Britain in 1871, Pineapple-weed grows in wasteground and trampled paths throughout Scotland. It has tufted leaves resembling Mayweed but with a *fruity smell when crushed*, and button-like, *greenish-yellow flowerheads, lacking ray florets* and less than 1 cm across.

Gael: Lus Anainn ('Pineapple Plant')

Corn Marigold

Chrysanthemum segetum
DAISY FAMILY

Probably a long-standing intro-duction from the Mediterranean with grain, Corn Marigold has become rarer in arable fields with the use of cleaner seed corn and herbicides, and is now most frequent in croft fields in NW Scotland and the W Isles, or more occasionally where a field corner is left unsprayed in the lowlands (see p. 18). It has yellow daisy *flowers*, with spreading ray florets, *up to 6 cm across*, and *toothed or lobed, rather bluish-green leaves*, at least the upper of which *half-clasp the stem*, which stands to 60 cm tall.

Gael: *Bile Bhuidhe (possibly 'Yellow Lip' or 'Yellow Leaf')*

Prickly Sow-thistle

Sonchus asper
DAISY FAMILY

This is marginally the commonest of 3 Sow-thistles in Scotland, all tall plants of cultivated land and wasteground around lowland areas, with rather spiny leaves, yellow dandelion-like heads and stems which exude a milky juice when cut. Prickly Sow-thistle has *hairless stems* and *glossy-green leaves*, with *spiny margins* and *rounded, back-projected basal lobes* (auricles). Its *flowers* are *deep golden-yellow*.

Gael: *Searbhan Muice ('Pig's Bitter One')*

OTHER SPECIES: Perennial Sow-thistle (*S. arvensis*) is similar, but with a *dense cover of yellow glandular hairs* on its upper stem and bracts. Smooth Sow-thistle (*S. oleraceus*) has *hairless stems, dull-green leaves lacking spines* and with *pointed, spreading auricles*, and *paler yellow flowers*.

THISTLES

Thistles (like Welted Thistle; right) are recognisable by their spiny, lobed leaves and bulbous flowerheads, which are usually purple (although occasionally white in some species). These lack ray-florets, but consist of a cluster of deeply-divided tubular florets. The swollen flower base is clothed in sepal-like bracts which are often spiny. The pip-like fruits are spread on tufts of feathery, branched hairs in the genus *Cirsium* or undivided, bristly hairs in the genus *Carduus*. There is much academic debate on which thistle is the Scottish emblem, but most probably this was chosen for the fierce armature of an undifferentiated, archetypal thistle.

Creeping Thistle

Cirsium arvense
DAISY FAMILY

One of 3 thistles that are omnipresent in fields, waysides and wasteground, this spreads by far-creeping roots which produce many leafy or flowering shoots, making the plant a serious agricultural pest. Its *stems are grooved, without leafy wings* and stand to around 90 cm in height. Its leaves are stalkless, variably-lobed and prickly and its *inflorescences have many, rather small, dullish-purple flowerheads* (up to 2.5 cm long). The bulbous *flower base has many, egg-shaped bracts pressed tightly around it, but with the outer, spine-tipped bracts spreading outwards.*

Gael: Fòthannan Achaidh ('Field Thistle')

OTHER SPECIES: Slender Thistle (*C. tenuiflorus*) with *cylindrical heads of pale purple flowers* and Musk Thistle (*C. nutans*) with *large, solitary, nodding flowerheads* grow near the coast in SE Scotland.

Spear Thistle

Cirsium vulgare
DAISY FAMILY

Another widespread and abundant species, this is distinguished by its *spiny-winged, grooved, cottony stems* to 1.5 m tall, *prickly-hairy leaves* with *spear-shaped lobes ending in a stout spine*, and *larger flowerheads* (to 5 cm long), which are *solitary or 2-3 in a group*. The *florets* are usually a *redder purple* and the *bracts* around the flower base are *narrow, spreading and spine-tipped*.

Gael: *Cluaran Deilgneach ('Prickly Thistle')*

Marsh Thistle

Cirsium palustre
DAISY FAMILY

The third common Scottish thistle, this grows in wetter ground including marshes and damp grassland. Its cottony *stem* stands to 1.5 m with a *continuous spiny wing*. Its *leaves* are *hairy above, narrowly-lobed*, spine-tipped and often *purple-bordered*, and its *smaller, dark reddish-purple (or frequently white) flowerheads*, to 2 cm long, with purplish, pointed but *not spine-tipped bracts*, are borne in *crowded, leafy clusters*.

Gael: *Cluaran Lèana (as English)*

Welted Thistle

Carduus crispus
DAISY FAMILY

Confined mainly to wasteground in the E lowlands, Welted Thistle (illustrated in box top left) has gangling, branched, cottony *stems* with *spiny wings stopping just beneath the flowerheads*. The clustered *heads, broader and redder* than those of Marsh Thistle, are surrounded by *spreading, narrow, green bracts* ending in a *weak spine*.

Gael: *Fòthannan Baltach ('Baltic Thistle')*

Globeflower

Trollius europaeus
BUTTERCUP FAMILY

Buttercup-like from a distance, Globeflower is easily distinguished by its *globe-shaped flowers*, to 3 cm across. The 5-15 golden-yellow *'petals'* (which are strictly sepals!) *completely enclose* the inner flower, so that only small insects can penetrate to fertilise it. The plant stands to 60 cm tall, with leaves that are roundish in outline but *deeply cut into 3-5 spreading, toothed and divided lobes.* It forms occasional patches in upland meadows in the Highlands and Borders (see p. 247), especially by rivers, and on mountain cliff-ledges, but is absent from the Isles except as a rare garden outcast on Shetland.
Gael: *Leolaicheann (perhaps 'Golden Ball')*

Common Whitlow-grass

Erophila verna
CABBAGE FAMILY

Common Whitlow-grass is a tiny, short-lived, spring-flowered annual of dry, open grassland, rocks and dunes in all but NW Scotland and the Isles. It has a *basal rosette of lance-shaped, slightly toothed leaves*, a short, leafless flowering stem and a branched inflorescence of white flowers, *up to 6 mm across*, with 4 *deeply-notched petals.* These ripen into *flattened, oval fruit-pods*, which leave a silver, papery sheath after splitting to shed their seeds.
Gael: *Biolradh Gruagain ('Hairy Dainty-one')*

OTHER SPECIES: Two closely-related species, with a similar range, are separated only on their degree of hairiness and petal division.

VIOLET FAMILY

Violets and pansies (like Wild Pansy; right) have toothed, usually heart-shaped leaves and flowers borne singly on long stalks. The flowers have 2 top petals projecting upwards, 2 equally-sized side petals and an enlarged lower petal, which is often marked with lines guiding insects to nectar in the long tube-like spur behind the lowest petal.

Wild Pansy

Viola tricolor
VIOLET FAMILY

This annual or perennial (illustrated above) grows in grassland and cultivated ground around most of Scotland, except for the C and NW Highlands. It resembles Field Pansy (p. 50) but has larger flowers (*to 25 mm vertically*), with *petals longer than the sepals* and coloured any combination of *purple, yellow and white*. The *spur* is *twice the length of the flaps at the base of the sepals*.
Gael: Goirmean-searradh (Goirmean = 'Blue One'; searradh obscure)

Common Dog-violet

Viola riviniana
VIOLET FAMILY

Called 'dogs' because they lack scent, Dog-violets have *more infolded flowers* than the flat 'faces' of pansies. This spring-flowered species, common in woods, hedgebanks, heaths, and grassland throughout Scotland, is distinguished by its *generally hairless, heart-shaped leaves* and *pale violet spur*, notched at its tip.
Gael: Dail-chuach ('Field Bowl')

OTHER SPECIES: Heath Dog-violet (V. canina) with *bluer flowers*, a *greenish-yellow spur* and *narrow triangular leaves* grows in scattered heaths and fens. Hairy Violet (V. hirta), with *hairy leaf-stalks* and *pale blue-violet flowers* is rare in coastal grassland in the SE.

Perforate
St. John's-wort

Hypericum perforatum
ST. JOHN'S-WORT FAMILY

One of several similar perennials, to 1 m in height, with opposite, oval leaves and clusters of yellow, 5-petalled flowers with numerous stamens, this species is distinguished by its *narrow leaves peppered with translucent, glandular dots* (best seen against the light) and stems with *2 raised lines*. It grows in grassland, woods and hedgebanks in the S.

Gael: Beachnuadh Boireann (*Boireann = female; first element obscure*)

OTHER SPECIES: Imperforate St. John's-wort (*H. maculatum*) with *black-dotted petals* and *square, unwinged stems* is uncommon in damp woodland. Square-stemmed St. John's-wort (*H. tetrapterum*), with *winged, 4-angled stems* grows in damp meadows in the S. Hairy St. John's-wort (*H. hirsutum*), with *hairy stems and leaves*, grows in damp woods and meadows in the E.

Common
Rock-rose

Helianthemum nummularium
ROCK-ROSE FAMILY

The only Scottish member of a mostly Mediterranean family, Rock-rose grows on grassy lime-rich banks in S and E Scotland (see p. 234). A low-growing *shrub* with trailing stems to 30 cm long, it has *opposite pairs of narrow, oval leaves* with a *white down* underneath. In summer it has showy, shining yellow, 5-petalled flowers, about 2 cm across, *with many stamens*.

The leaf shape distinguishes it from cinquefoils with similar flowers.

Gael: Grian-ròs ('Sun Rose')

Maiden Pink

Dianthus deltoides
PINK FAMILY

This delicate perennial grows on lime-rich grassy banks, especially near limestone or in sand-dunes. Rarely exceeding 20 cm in height, with *narrow, blue-green, rough-edged leaves*, it is easily overlooked amongst tall grass despite its attractive *flowers* in summer. These are *blushing pink* (hence the common name), usually with a *pale centre surrounded by a darker pink band*, and with *petals frayed at their tips*. 2-4 broad bracts enclose the flowers outside a tube of 5 sepals. The only wild Scottish pink, it is restricted to the SE, but declining through overgrazing or scrub encroachment.

Gael: Pinc ('Pink'!)

Fairy Flax

Linum catharcticum
FLAX FAMILY

This slender annual is found virtually throughout Scotland, although nowhere abundantly, in grassland, heaths and dunes usually on base-rich soils. Its *unbranched, wiry stems* rarely exceed 15 cm, with *opposite, oblong leaves*. Its small *flowers, about 8 mm across*, are borne in *widely-branched inflorescences* in summer. They have 5 sepals, *5 narrow, white petals* and 5 stamens. It is sometimes called Purging Flax from its former herbal use as a purgative.

Gael: Lìon nam Ban-sìdh ('Fairy Women's Flax' – see Foxglove; p. 38)

OTHER SPECIES: The *tall, blue-flowered* Cultivated Flax (*L. usitatissimum*) is occasionally grown for linseed oil production.

67

Bloody Cranesbill

Geranium sanguineum
CRANESBILL FAMILY

The most striking of the Cranesbills (p. 26), this species is named after its *rich purplish-crimson flowers* which appear in midsummer. These are up to *3 cm across*, with *shallowly notched petals*, and are usually *solitary* on long stalks. The plant has a rather *bushy form* to 40 cm tall, with spreading, hairy stems. Its *leaves* are rounded in outline, 2-6 cm across but *deeply cut* into many *narrow, rather pointed* lobes. It grows uncommonly on lime-rich rocks and sand-dunes, mostly near the coast in S Scotland, but also around the Moray Firth, and on Mull, Coll and Tiree.

Gael: Creachlach Dearg (possibly 'Red Wound-healer')

Tufted Vetch

Vicia cracca
PEA FAMILY

Vetches typically are climbing or scrambling plants, with leaves divided into many pairs of opposite leaflets and ending in a tendril which twines round neighbouring plants for support. They usually have clusters of purplish pea flowers (p. 71). This species conforms to the norm, and is identified by its *handsome, one-sided, densely-flowered spike in summer of up to 40 blue-violet flowers, 8-12 mm long*, and its *slightly hairy leaves*, which have *6-12 pairs of narrow oval, shortly-pointed leaflets*, and end in a *branched tendril*. It is common in grassy or bushy places all round Scotland, except for wilder areas of the Highlands.

Gael: Peasair nan Luch ('Mice's Pea')

Bush Vetch

Vicia sepium
PEA FAMILY

Reminiscent of the previous species, this is distinguished by its *hairless leaves* with 5-9 pairs of *broad egg-shaped leaflets* ending in a *branched tendril*. Its less showy inflorescences in spring and summer have 2-6, *pale purple flowers* which are 12-15 mm long. It is widespread in rough grassland, hedges and thickets around virtually all of Scotland.

Gael: Peasair nam Preas ('Bush Pea')

Common Vetch

Vicia sativa
PEA FAMILY

More variable than the previous 2 perennials, this is a tufted, slightly hairy, sprawling *annual*, found in hedges, grassy places and sand-dunes around the lowlands and NE, but not in most of the Highlands or Islands. Its leaves have 3-8 pairs of *narrow leaflets* and end in a *branched or unbranched tendril*, and its *reddish purple flowers*, up to 2 cm long, are usually *solitary or paired* at the base of a leaf. As a final check, the *leafy appendage* at the base of the leaf stalk has a *black blotch on its underside*. More robust, larger-flowered forms, with broader leaflets, are sometimes grown for fodder.

Gael: Peasair nan Coilleag (for wild form) ('Sand-dune Pea')

OTHER SPECIES: Hairy Tare (*V. hirsuta*), a slender annual with insignificant, *lilac-tinged flowers about 5 mm long* and *4-8 pairs of narrow leaflets*, grows in grassy places in the lowlands and Moray Firth area, and as a rare casual in the N Isles.

Meadow Vetchling

Lathyrus pratensis
PEA FAMILY

Peas and vetchlings (*Lathyrus* species) differ from vetches in having *winged or angled stems* and *fewer pairs of leaflets*. This is the commonest vetchling, found in grassland and hedges throughout Scotland, although rare in the NW. It is the only vetchling with *yellow flowers*, which are about 15 mm long and in clusters of *5-12*. It has scrambling, *sharply-angled stems*, sometimes over 1 m long, and *downy leaves* with a *single pair* of *lance-shaped leaflets* and a *branched or unbranched tendril* at the tip. At the base of the leaf stalk, there is a pair of *leafy, arrow-shaped appendages* (stipules).
Gael: *Peasair Bhuidhe* ('Yellow Pea')

Bitter Vetch

Lathyrus linifolius
PEA FAMILY

Lower-growing and with *winged stems*, Bitter Vetch(ling) has *reddish-purple flowers* in spring and early summer, later *fading to blue*. Its *hairless leaves* have 2-4 pairs of *narrowly lance-shaped leaflets* but lack tendrils, which are replaced by a short, green point. The *stipules* at the base of the leaf-stalks are *lance-shaped and toothed*. The plant is common in woods, hedgebanks and heaths throughout Scotland.
Gael: *Cairt Leamhna* (perhaps 'Elm Bark' – derivation unclear)

OTHER SPECIES: Sea Pea (*L. japonicus*) with *purple flowers, angled stems*, and *leaves with 3-4 oval leaflets and tendrils*, grows in a single Shetland sand-dune.

THE PEA FLOWER

Flowers of the pea family, like those of Common Birdsfoot-trefoil (right), characteristically have a broad upper petal (the 'standard'), 2 narrower side petals ('wings'), and 2 lower petals united at their base to form a boat-like 'keel'. Pollination is by heavy insects, such as bees, which land on and weigh down the keel, to reach the pollen.

Common Restharrow

Ononis repens
PEA FAMILY

'Restharrow' records the tough, creeping underground stems, which once brought horse-drawn harrows to a halt. This is the only Scottish species, found in rough grassland and sand-dunes in the E lowlands and near W coasts. It has *hairy, shrubby stems* to 60 cm tall, sometimes with soft, weak spines, leaves with 3 (sometimes 1) rounded, *downy, toothed leaflets*, and *pink flowers*, 10-15 mm long, in summer.

Gael: Sreang Bogha ('Bowstring')

Black Medick

Medicago lupulina
PEA FAMILY

This low, downy annual has a similar range to Restharrow in grassy places and roadsides. Its leaves have *3 broad leaflets* ending in a *minute point*. In summer, it has round heads of 10-50 tiny, *deep yellow flowers* (about 3 mm long), which develop into *kidney-shaped pods*, turning black when ripe.

Gael: Dubh-mheidig (as English)

White Clover

Trifolium repens
PEA FAMILY

Clovers are low-growing annuals or perennials with *trefoil leaves* (i.e. with 3 leaflets) and *dense heads* of many small, stalkless flowers with *wings longer than their keel* (see pea flower, p. 71). White Clover is abundant in grassy places throughout the country, and is sometimes planted for its soil-enriching root bacteria. It has *creeping, rooting stems*, and *toothed leaflets*, usually with a *pale band* towards their base. The roundish flowerhead in summer contains 40-80 *white or pale pink flowers*, which have a *white sepal-tube* marked with *green veins* and ending in teeth about half as long as the tube.

Gael: Seamrag Bhàn (as English)

OTHER SPECIES: Alsike Clover (*T. hybridum*), with *large heads of whitish flowers* but *without creeping stems or white-blotched leaves* is naturalised in grassy places in the lowlands.

Red Clover

Trifolium pratense
PEA FAMILY

Widespread throughout Scottish grassland, Red Clover *lacks creeping stems* and has *globe-shaped* heads of *pinkish-purple flowers*. Its leaves have *narrowly oval leaflets*, which are usually marked with a *whitish crescent* and are *hairy beneath*, and *oblong stipules* ending in a *bristle*.

Gael: Seamrag Dhearg (as English)

OTHER SPECIES: Zigzag Clover (*T. medium*), a much less common species of lowland grasslands, has narrow *leaflets* with only a *faint white spot*, *narrow stipules*, and *reddish-purple flowers* in flattened heads.

Haresfoot Clover

Trifolium arvense
PEA FAMILY

The flowers of this softly hairy annual have *sepals* ending in *long, bristly hairs*, which give the inflorescence a *fluffy appearance* reminiscent of some grasses and supposedly like a hare's foot. The sepal bristles completely hide the *white or pink flowers* which are only 4 mm long. The plant grows to 20 cm, with spreading branches and narrow, hairy leaflets. It inhabits sandy fields, grassland and dunes, mostly near coasts, in S Scotland and the Moray Firth area.

Gael: *Cas Maighiche ('Hare's Foot')*

OTHER SPECIES: Knotted Clover (*T. striatum*), with *downy leaves* and *fluffy, pinkish flowerheads enfolded by leaf-stipules*, is uncommon in open grassland in the E.

Lesser Trefoil

Trifolium dubium
PEA FAMILY

The commonest *yellow-flowered* Scottish clover, this annual has *long-stalked, rounded heads*, about *7 mm across*, of 3-15 tiny flowers, in the angles of its upper leaves. Its stems can trail for 20 cm, and its leaves have 3, *oval leaflets* and *oval stipules*. It resembles Black Medick (p.71), but has *hairless* (not downy) *leaves* and sepals, and its *leaflets* are *slightly notched at the tip*.

Gael: *Seangan ('(Little) Slender One')*

OTHER SPECIES: Hop Trefoil (*T. campestre*), resembling Lesser Trefoil but with *erect stems* and *flowerheads to 15 mm across* with *20-30 flowers*, grows in grassy lowland areas.

Common Birdsfoot-trefoil

Lotus corniculatus
PEA FAMILY

A ubiquitous, *hairless* perennial of grasslands throughout Scotland, Birdsfoot-trefoil actually has *5 leaflets*, but the lowest 2 are *attached to the stem*, like stipules, leaving 3 free (trefoil) lobes. Its *solid stems* creep along the ground, forming spreading patches, with heads of 2-6 flowers (see p. 71) on stout flower-stalks in summer, developing into pods which spread like birds' claws. The yellow flowers are streaked with red, especially in bud, hence the dialect name 'bacon-and-eggs'.
Gael: Peasair a' Mhadaidh-ruaidh ('Fox's Pea')

OTHER SPECIES: Greater Birdsfoot-trefoil (*L. pedunculatus*), with *hollow stems, hairy leaves,* and *usually 8 or more flowers* in a head, grows in damp grassland in S Scotland.

Silverweed

Potentilla anserina
ROSE FAMILY

The only common yellow flower with *silvery compound leaves*, Silverweed is a perennial of damp grassland, sand-dunes and roadsides in all but the C Highlands. It spreads by *creeping, rooting stems*, producing regular rosettes of leaves, up to 25 cm long, with 7-12 pairs of main leaflets, alternating with smaller ones, and a terminal leaflet. The *leaflets* are *egg-shaped, toothed and silky with hairs,* especially below. The showy summer flowers, with 5 yellow petals, are 2 cm or more across.
Gael: Brisgean ('Brittle One')

Tormentil

Potentilla erecta
ROSE FAMILY

A perennial of grassland, heaths, bogs, woods and mountainsides throughout Scotland, Tormentil has yellow, *4-petalled* (occasionally 3- or 5-petalled) *flowers, less than 1 cm across,* and leaves with 3 (occasionally 4 or 5) *spreading, toothed leaflets.* Its slender, flexuous stems, 10-30 cm tall, arise from a thick, creeping, woody stock, but *do not develop independent roots.*
Gael: Cairt-làir ('Ground Bark')

OTHER SPECIES: Creeping Cinquefoil (*P. reptans*) with 5 *leaflets* and *flowers to 2.5 cm across,* spreads by *rooting runners* in hedgebanks and waste places in the S. Trailing Tormentil (*P. anglica*) is intermediate between the previous 2, with *trailing flower-stems* which *root in late summer,* and *4- and 5-petalled flowers on the same plant;* it is rarer in hedgebanks and heathland in the S.

Common Lady's-mantle

Alchemilla vulgaris
ROSE FAMILY

The name is used here for a group of similar perennials of grassland and open woods throughout Scotland except the far NW. All have round leaves in outline, with spreading, toothed *lobes, cut less than half-way into the leaf* (cf Alpine Lady's-mantle; p. 221). The variably-hairy *leaves* are *pleated when young* like a spreading cloak or mantle. The tiny *flowers,* in *dense clusters* in summer, have *no petals* but 4, *greenish-yellow sepals.*
Gael: Fallaing Moire ('Mary's Mantle')

Meadow Saxifrage

Saxifraga granulata
SAXIFRAGE FAMILY

The life-history of this *spring-flowered* saxifrage restricts it to well-established grassland. At the base of its rosette leaves, it produces *pinkish bulbils* (small buds) and only these, if not disturbed or heavily-grazed, survive to produce the next year's plants. Its *round-toothed, kidney-shaped, hairy leaves*, to 3 cm across, are mostly in a basal rosette, which sometimes withers before flowering, with few leaves up the *softly-hairy* stems. These are 10-50 cm tall, topped by a spreading head of white flowers, *up to 2 cm across*, with *broad, rounded petals*. It is found uncommonly in S and E Scotland.

Gael: *Moran (derivation obscure)*

Cowslip

Primula veris
PRIMROSE FAMILY

Cowslip is a decreasing, spring-flowered perennial of *base-rich* pastures, mostly in E Scotland, with a few sites in the W, along the N coast and in Orkney. It is closely related to Primrose (p. 139), but has up to 30 *nodding, deep-yellow flowers* in a spreading head on a *leafless, downy flower-stalk* to 30 cm tall. The flowers are *tubular*, with *short, inward-curved petal-lobes*. The downy, *oblong, gently-toothed leaves* narrow abruptly into a leaf-stalk.

Gael: *Mùisean (derivation obscure)*

Hybrids between Cowslip and Primrose are not uncommon within Cowslip's range. They are Cowslip-like, but have larger, paler yellow flowers and less abruptly-narrowed leaf bases.

Sheep's Sorrel

Rumex acetosella
DOCK FAMILY

A slender docken (p. 34) to 30 cm tall, with *arrow-shaped leaves*, Sheep's Sorrel is found in heathy and grassy places throughout Scotland, often on poor soils. It can survive heavy grazing on upland pastures because sheep avoid eating its bitter leaves. It is a perennial with a creeping rootstock which buds to produce new plants. Its narrow, arrow-shaped *leaves*, which are up to 4 cm long, have *upward-pointing lobes* at their base, and all are *distinctly stalked*. The reddish flowers are borne in well-spaced clusters from May to September in a leafless, slightly branched inflorescence.

Gael: *Sealbhag nan Caorach* (as English)

Common Sorrel

Rumex acetosa
DOCK FAMILY

Even more widespread in grassland, hedgebanks and woodland clearings, this is distinguished from Sheep's Sorrel by its *broader, lance-shaped leaves*, to 15 cm long, with *downwardly-directed basal lobes*. The upper leaves *clasp the stem*, which can be *up to 60 cm tall*. The *flower-spikes* are *broader and less sparse* than those of Sheep's Sorrel, and most are fruiting by August, after which the plant turns rich crimson. Both species have male and female flowers on separate plants.

Gael: *Sealbhag* ('Little Bitter One') or *Sàmh* ('Rest/Peace')

Common Sorrel is known as 'Sooracks' in much of Scotland from its acid-tasting leaves, which are sometimes eaten in salads. A red/brown dye was obtained from its roots.

77

Field Gentian

Gentianella campestris
GENTIAN FAMILY

Gentianella species are distinguished from 'true' gentians (*Gentiana* species) by the *fringe of hairs* in the mouth of their petal-tubes. Field Gentian, the commoner of 2 Scottish species, grows in pastures and dunes, mostly in the N and W. It is a hairless biennial with a slightly-branched stem, 10-30 cm tall, and lance-shaped leaves. Its flowers, which appear from July to October, have a *bluish-lilac (or occasionally white) petal-tube*, about 2 cm long, with 4 out-spread lobes. The *petals just overtop* the *sepal-tube*, which has *2 broad outer lobes almost hiding 2 narrower inner lobes*.
Gael: Lus a' Chrùbain ('The Crouching Plant')

Autumn Gentian

Gentianella amarella
GENTIAN FAMILY

Very similar to the previous species, Autumn Gentian has *deeper purple flowers* (occasionally pink, white or bluish) in *July and August*. Its *petal-tube* usually has *5 lobes* (sometimes with 4-lobed flowers on the same plant) and is *twice as long as the sepal-tube*. This has *4 or 5, equally-sized teeth* pressed against the petal-tube. The plant grows in lime-rich grassland and dunes around Scottish coasts and islands, and inland in the C and NW Highlands, but is generally rare in the W.
Gael: Lus a' Chrùbain Tuathach ('Northern Crouching Plant')

OTHER SPECIES: The *slender, blue-flowered* Alpine Gentian (*Gentiana nivalis*) is a very rare plant of a few high, lime-rich mountains.

Changing Forget-me-not

Myosotis discolor
BORAGE FAMILY

Whereas most Forget-me-nots have pink buds (p. 56), the *flowers* of this species *open yellow and turn blue*. This combination of young, yellow flowers near the tip of a curled inflorescence and blue flowers lower down distinguishes it from any other plant. It is a spring- and summer-flowered annual, little more than 10 cm tall, with *hairy stems and leaves*, and *flower-stalks shorter than its sepal-tubes*. It grows in open grassland, scattered throughout Scotland, including the Isles.

Gael: *Lus Midhe Caochlaideach* ('Changing Midhe Plant' (midhe obscure))

OTHER SPECIES: Early Forget-me-not (*M. ramosissima*), the only other Forget-me-not with *flower-stalks shorter than sepal-tubes*, has *spring flowers* only 2 mm across, *pink in bud*, and grows in dry grassland and dunes, mostly near E coasts.

Viper's Bugloss

Echium vulgare
BORAGE FAMILY

This handsome biennial grows on sea-cliffs, dunes, and light soils only a little inland in the S and NE. It has stout stems to 90 cm tall, and roughly *hairy*, lance-shaped *leaves* with a *prominent midrib*, the lower ones stalked and the upper *clasping the stem*. In summer it produces spikes of *blue flowers* (pink in bud), funnel-shaped with a *prominent lower lip*, and 1 or more *pink stamens projecting from the flower's open throat*.

Gael: *Lus na Nathrach* ('Adder's Plant')

SPEEDWELLS

17 speedwells are found in Scotland. 2 species live in the mountains, 4 in wet areas and 11 in lowland fields and grasslands. All have a petal-tube with 4 lobes, of which the uppermost is the largest (representing 2 united petals) and the lowest is often narrower. Two stamens and 1 style protrude from the mouth of the petal-tube. Most have blue flowers, often with prominent blue lines guiding insects to their pollen.

Heath Speedwell

Veronica officinalis
SPEEDWELL FAMILY

This mat-forming perennial (illustrated above) is widespread in heaths, grassland and open woods throughout Scotland, including the Isles. It flowers in summer, producing *small, pale-lilac flowers* in a *dense, leafless spike*. Its *leaves are oval and hairy*.
Gael: Lus-crè Monaidh ('Heath Dust-plant')

Germander Speedwell

Veronica chamaedrys
SPEEDWELL FAMILY

This is the most widespread Scottish speedwell, forming sprawling patches in grassland and woods, although in Shetland and the W Isles it is an uncommon relict of cultivation. It is a perennial, with *toothed, egg-shaped, hairy leaves*, and *2 lines of long white hairs down opposite sides* of its weak stems. In spring and summer, it produces *deep blue flowers* with a *prominent white 'eye'*, on long stalks from the upper leaves.
Gael: An-uallach ('Unproud', ie 'Humble')

Thyme-leaved Speedwell

Veronica serpyllifolia
SPEEDWELL FAMILY

Another widespread perennnial, this flowers throughout spring and summer in damp grassland, heaths, and disturbed ground, including gardens. Its *flowers* are *white or pale blue with darker lines*, borne in the angle of the upper stem leaves. Its *leaves* are *oblong and hairless* and its creeping *stems root along their length*. A subspecies with larger, bluer flowers grows in wet mountain grassland.

Gael: Lus-crè Talmhainn ('Ground Dust-plant')

OTHER SPECIES: Ivy-leaved Speedwell (V. *hederifolia*), with similar flowers but *kidney-shaped leaves*, grows in cultivated ground, mostly in the E. Slender speedwell (V. *filiformis*), a garden escape, forms sheets of *pale lilac-blue flowers* on *thread-like stalks* in disturbed lowland grassland.

Common Field Speedwell

Veronica persica
SPEEDWELL FAMILY

This *annual* produces *bright-blue flowers*, with a *paler bottom lobe*, almost throughout the year in lowland fields and waste ground. It has *hairy, branched, rather straggling stems* and *egg-shaped leaves*.

Gael: Lus-crè Gàrraidh ('Garden Dust-plant')

OTHER SPECIES: The rather similar, annual Wall Speedwell (V. *arvensis*) is distinguished by its *tiny, bright-blue flowers* (*rarely exceeding 3 mm across*). Despite its common name, it grows in open or cultivated ground.

Yellow Rattle

Rhinanthus minor
FIGWORT FAMILY

This variable annual, with several sub-species, grows in grassland throughout Scotland. Like many of its family, it lives as a partial parasite, its roots tapping into other plants' roots for nourishment. It has branched or unbranched, often *black-spotted stems* to 50 cm tall, opposite pairs of *narrow, toothed, strongly-veined leaves*, and *leafy spikes* of yellow flowers in late spring and summer. The *flowers* are 15-20 mm long, with an *inflated sepal-tube* with 4 teeth, and a 2-lipped petal-tube. The upper lip is *flattened sideways, enclosing 4 stamens*, and the lower lip is *3-lobed*.

Gael: Modhalan Buidhe (possibly 'Yellow Modest One')

Eyebright

Euphrasia officinalis
FIGWORT FAMILY

Abundant partial parasites of grassland throughout Scotland, Eyebrights are a group of many, near-identical 'microspecies', several of which are endemic (exclusive) to Scotland. All are low-growing annuals, with *toothed, often purplish, oval leaves*, and spikes of *white or purplish flowers* in summer. These have a *4-toothed sepal-tube* and a 2-lipped petal-tube. The upper lip of this is *curved backwards* and often etched with purple lines, and the lower lip is *strongly 3-lobed, blotched with yellow* near the throat and often purple veined.

Gael: Lus nan Leac ('Plant of the Hillsides')

The name comes from the flowers, which supposedly look like shining eyes and so were used in herbal eye-baths.

Red Bartsia

Odontites vernus
FIGWORT FAMILY

Another partial parasite of grassland, Red Bartsia is found in S Scotland and near coasts in the N and Isles. It is a *downy, often purple-tinted* annual, variably branched and up to 30 cm tall, with *toothed, narrow, spear-shaped leaves*. Its *purplish-pink*, midsummer *flowers* are about 8 mm long, all *bending towards one side* of a dense, *leafy spike*. It has a *4-toothed sepal-tube* and a *2-lipped petal-tube* in which the upper lip forms an *open hood* and the lower lip is *3-lobed*.

Gael: Modhalan Coitcheann (possibly 'Common Modest One')

OTHER SPECIES: Alpine Bartsia (*Bartsia alpina*), a rare plant of base-rich mountains in the C Highlands, has *broader leaves* and *hairy, deep purple flowers* surrounded by *purple bracts*.

Wild Thyme

Thymus polytrichus
THYME FAMILY

Although its scientific name has changed regularly, this is the only Scottish thyme, growing in dry grassland, heaths and dunes throughout the country. A low, *mat-forming shrub*, it has squarish *stems* with *long hairs on 2 sides*, and *opposite, leathery, oval leaves* which are *aromatic* when crushed. In summer, it produces *domed heads* of *rosy-purple flowers* with a *hairy, 2-lipped sepal-tube*. The *petals* also form a 2-lipped tube, with a *strongly 3-lobed* lower lip, a slightly 2-lobed upper lip, and *4 protruding stamens*.

Gael: Lus an Rìgh ('The King's Plant')

83

Selfheal

Prunella vulgaris
THYME FAMILY

The *stalked, pointed, oval, slightly toothed leaves* of this abundant, patch-forming, *downy* perennial are found in lawns, grassland and woodland clearings throughout Scotland. It has squarish flowering stems, to 30 cm tall, topped in summer by *dense, oblong heads* of *violet flowers* (more rarely pink or white) *with leaf-like bracts below each*. The bracts, like the 2-lipped sepal-tube, are *often purple-tinged* with *long white hairs*. The flowers have 2 lips, the lower of which is 3-lobed and the upper strongly hooded.

Gael: Dubhan Ceann-chòsach (possibly 'Spongy-headed Kidney')
The plant was considered a powerful treatment for external and internal wounds – hence 'self-heal'.

Bugle

Ajuga reptans
THYME FAMILY

Somewhat reminiscent of Self heal, Bugle has *hairless*, more rounded and *scarcely toothed leaves*, with the *upper leaves and bracts almost stalkless* and often purplish. It has unbranched stems, to 30 cm tall, which are *usually hairy on 2 sides*. It flowers slightly earlier, *in spring and early summer*, producing dense, leafy spikes of *violet-blue, veined flowers*. These have a strongly 3-lobed lower lip, but the upper lip is *short and inconspicuous*, apparently replaced by the 4 blue stamens. Bugle grows in damp grassland and woods, but is uncommon in the N and Isles. (cf Water Mint, p. 174)

Gael: Glasair Choille ('Green One of the Wood')

Ground Ivy

Glechoma hederacea
THYME FAMILY

This *hairy*, patch-forming perennial is common in grassland, woodland and hedgebanks in S and E Scotland, but is absent from much of the N and W and the W Isles, and only a rare garden outcast in the N Isles. Its *stems* creep over the ground, *rooting along their length*, with *long-stalked, kidney-shaped, roundly-toothed leaves*, only slightly resembling ivy. In *springtime*, well-separated whorls of *2-4 blue-violet flowers* develop in the angles of leaf-like bracts. The lower lip of the flowers is *spotted with deeper purple* and the upper is *flat* (not incurved).

Gael: Eidheann Thalmhainn (as English)

Scottish Bluebell

Campanula rotundifolia
BELLFLOWER FAMILY

Although 'officially' called Harebell, this delicate, hairless perennial is usually known as Bluebell in Scotland. It grows in dry grassland, sand-dunes, machair and rock-ledges throughout Scotland, but is less common in the NW and rare in the N Isles. Its thin underground runners produce open patches of slender stems, 15-40 cm tall. The round leaves of the scientific name are the easily-overlooked long-stalked root leaves (shown above); its more obvious stem *leaves* are *narrow and grass-like*. It flowers in *mid to late summer*, producing a spreading group of *nodding, blue, broadly bell-shaped flowers*, *about 15 mm long*.

Gael: Currac-cuthaige ('Cuckoo's-cap')

85

Sheepsbit

Jasione montana
BELLFLOWER FAMILY

Members of the Bellflower family have petals united into a bell-shaped tube, but in Sheepsbit this is deeply divided into 5 *narrow lobes*, giving a tufted appearance to the *crowded, roundish heads* of small, *blue flowers*. The plant is a *downy* biennial, with spreading stems to 50 cm tall and narrow, *wavy, untoothed leaves*, the upper of which are *unstalked*. It grows in grassland, heaths and sea cliffs, mostly in the SW, more rarely in the E, but commonly in Shetland. It is separated from similar-looking scabiouses (p.89) by its *anthers*, which are *joined at their base into a short tube.*

Gael: *Putan Gorm* ('*Blue Button*')

Common Valerian

Valeriana officinalis
VALERIAN FAMILY

A rather variable, *strong-smelling* perennial, Common Valerian has usually unbranched stems 20-150 cm tall, which are hairy only at their base. Its opposite, paired leaves are divided into *several pairs of oval, toothed leaflets* with a single terminal leaflet. In summer, its stems are topped by umbrella-like clusters of *tiny, pale-pink flowers* (darker in bud) with their petals united into a *funnel-shaped* tube, about 5 mm across and enclosing *3 stamens*. Valerian grows in rough grassland, scrub and marshes over most of Scotland, but becomes sparser in the N and is absent from Shetland.

Gael: *Carthan Curaidh* (*perhaps 'Warrior's Friendship'*)

Ribwort Plantain

Plantago lanceolata
PLANTAIN FAMILY

Plantains are familiar weeds with a basal rosette of ribbed or veined leaves, leafless flowering stems, and dense elongated spikes of tiny flowers with reduced petals and sepals but prominent, rather showy stamens. Ribwort Plantain, an abundant species of grassy places throughout Scotland, has *narrow, lance-shaped leaves*, 2-30 cm long, with *3-5 prominent veins*. Its *deeply-grooved stalks* are about twice as long as the leaves, and are topped by a *dumpy, egg-shaped inflorescence, up to 5 cm long*. The flowers are fertile, with ripe anthers displayed, in spring and early summer.

Gael: Slàn-lus (perhaps 'Healing Plant')

Greater Plantain

Plantago major
PLANTAIN FAMILY

Even more widespread than the previous species, Greater Plantain grows in disturbed ground, including lawns, gardens, fields, roadsides and wasteground throughout Scotland. It has *broader, oval, usually hairless leaves*, with *3-9 veins*. The leaves are 5-15 cm long, with *stalks as long as their blades*. The narrow *inflorescence*, fertile in *summer*, is *10-15 cm long* and takes up most of the *unfurrowed stem*.

Gael: Cuach Phàdraig ('Patrick's Cup')

OTHER SPECIES: Hoary Plantain (*P. media*), an uncommon plant of richer grassland in the E, has similarly shaped but *short-stalked, greyish, and softly hairy leaves* and *scented flowers* with conspicuous *anthers* which are *purple when young*. (See also pp. 109 and 110).

Lady's Bedstraw

Galium verum
BEDSTRAW FAMILY

The commoner of 2 yellow-flowered Bedstraws (see below), this species grows, sometimes abundantly, in grassland, hedgebanks, machair and sand-dunes throughout Scotland, although less commonly in the NW. A typical bedstraw (p. 40), it has *sprawling, 4-angled stems*, to 60 cm or more in length, which *turn black when dried*. Its *narrow, needle-like leaves*, in whorls of 8-12, are usually *hairless*, with incurled margins. It has *golden-yellow flowers* in dense, fluffy heads at the top of the stem in late summer.

Gael: Lus an Leasaich ('Rennet Plant') or Ruadhain ('red' – from dye)
Its foliage, smelling of new-mown hay when dried was once gathered for fresh-scented bedding and is said to have been used at the Nativity, hence 'Our Lady's Bedstraw'. Its roots yield a red dye.

Crosswort

Cruciata laevipes
BEDSTRAW FAMILY

The only other yellow-flowered Bedstraw, Crosswort is different enough to be placed in a separate genus. Its *broader, oval, softly hairy leaves*, with *3 prominent veins*, are arranged in *cross-like whorls of 4* up its scrambling stems, which are 15-60 cm long. In spring and early summer, it produces tiny, 4-petalled flowers, 2-3 mm in diameter, *tightly clustered into the angles of its upper leaves (bracts)* like flowers in a basket. It is a plant of lime-rich grassland, roadsides and open woodland, confined mainly to S Scotland.

Gael: Lus na Croise ('Plant of the Cross')

Field Scabious

Knautia arvensis
TEASEL FAMILY

This *roughly hairy* perennial stands up to 1 m tall, with stem leaves mostly *deeply-cut* into narrow lobes, although some upper leaves may be undivided. Its small flowers, in late summer, are borne in *dense, rounded heads*, about 3 cm in diameter, surrounded by *2 rings of narrow, hairy bracts*. The *bluish-lilac petals* are united into a 4-lobed tube, with the *enlarged outer lobes* of the outermost flowers forming a *slight frill round the inflorescence*. It grows in dry pastures, mostly in E Scotland.

Gael: *Gille Guirmein* ('Blue Lad')

OTHER SPECIES: Small Scabious (*Scabiosa columbaria*), with *more divided leaves, deeper blue, 5-lobed flowers* and a *single row of bracts*, is rare in lime-rich grassland in the far S and Angus.

Devil's-bit Scabious

Succisa pratensis
TEASEL FAMILY

Generally smaller than Field Scabious (although up to 1 m tall), this has *undivided, narrowly oval* often purple-blotched *leaves*. It flowers in summer and early autumn in meadows, woods and marshland throughout Scotland, producing rounded heads, about *2 cm in diameter*, of *dark purplish-blue flowers, without any frill* of outer petal-lobes.

Gael: *Ura-bhallach* (derivation obscure)
The abruptly truncated rootstock is said to have been bitten off by the Devil out of spite for the root's herbal powers.

Yarrow

Achillea millefolium
DAISY FAMILY

One of the commonest grassland species throughout Scotland, Yarrow is easily recognised by its *feathery leaves* which are lance-shaped in outline but *deeply cut into 'thousands' of fine segments* (hence *'millefolium'*). Grazing animals generally avoid the strong-smelling and bitter-tasting leaves, which are therefore often abundant in well-grazed pastures, spreading by underground stems. It flowers where less heavily grazed, producing *flattish, umbrella-like inflorescences* in summer, on top of *furrowed, woolly stems* to 45 cm tall. The small daisy flowerheads (p. 60) are about 5 mm across, with *usually 5 broad, white or pink rays* and a *creamy-white disc*.
Gael: *Eàrr-thalmhainn ('Tail of the Earth' or Eàrr may be from English)*
The scientific name honours Achilles who supposedly used this powerful herbal plant to heal wounds and treat fevers.

Sneezewort

Achillea ptarmica
DAISY FAMILY

The creamy-white flowers immediately show Sneezewort to be a relative of Yarrow, but the *flowerheads* are *bigger* (to 18 mm across), with *8-12 rays* and a *greenish-white disc*, and the *inflorescence* is *more open and fewer-flowered*. The *leaves* are also different: *lance-shaped, stalkless and undivided*, with a *fine, saw-toothed edge*. Sneezewort grows in damp grassland, marshes and streamsides, throughout Scotland but more scattered than Yarrow. It flowers from July to September.
Gael: *Cruaidh-lus ('Hard Weed')*

90

Ox-eye Daisy

Leucanthemum vulgare
DAISY FAMILY

Called Gowans or Horse Gowans in parts of Scotland, Ox-eye Daisy is common in grassland in the S and rarer in the N. It has solitary, typical daisy flowerheads, to 5 cm across, with white, petal-like rays, a yellow central disc, and oblong *bracts with narrow purple margins*. The plant somewhat resembles Scentless Mayweed (p. 60), but the *leaves* are *toothed* (not finely divided). The upper leaves are *oblong and stalkless*, half-clasping the stem, while the less obvious lower leaves are *spoon-shaped and long-stalked*. The slender, branched, hairless stems stand to 1 m tall.

Gael: Neòinean Mòr ('Big Daisy' – see Daisy; p. 23)

Melancholy Thistle

Cirsium heterophyllum
DAISY FAMILY

The only Scottish thistle *without deeply-lobed, spiny leaves*, this handsome perennial grows in hill pastures and streamsides in the Borders and Highlands (see p. 237). It can be over 1 m tall, with unbranched, *grooved, cottony stems*. Its *soft, bright green leaves* have a *dense white felt underneath*. They are usually *oblong and toothed*, although the lower leaves may be deeply cut into broad, forwardly-directed lobes. In midsummer, it produces purple flowerheads, 3-5 cm across, on an egg-shaped cup of purplish, spine-tipped bracts. The heads are either solitary (hence 'melancholy') or 2-3 in a closely-branching inflorescence.

Gael: Cluas an Fhèidh ('Deer's Ear')

Dandelion

Taraxacum officinale
DAISY FAMILY

The many, confusing dandelion-like plants are generally separable by the shape of leaves, inflorescence and bracts. Dandelions themselves (a group of over 200 closely-related 'microspecies') have *solitary flowerheads* on *unbranched, leafless stems*, 5-30 cm tall, which *exude milky juice* when cut. The *leaves*, in a *basal rosette*, are generally oblong and *deeply lobed*, with the lobes *curving downwards* like lions' teeth (*dent-de-lion*). The yellow flowerheads, which appear all year round but most abundantly in spring, have only ray florets and are 1.5-5.5 cm across, often with *down-curved bracts*. The *beaked fruits* have a *tuft of hairs* for dispersal. Dandelions grow in grassland, wasteground and marshes throughout Scotland.

Gael: Beàrnan Bride ('St. Bride's Notched One')

Cat's-ear

Hypochoeris radicata
DAISY FAMILY

Widespread in grassland, waysides and dunes, Cat's-ear has a *basal rosette* of *roughly hairy*, toothed or lobed *leaves*. Its *leafless and hairless stems*, to 60 cm tall, are usually *forked* and *lack milky juice*. The stems are *swollen* and *covered in scale-like bracts* beneath the *flowerheads*, which are 2-4 cm across, with *pointed scales between the florets*. The outer *ray-florets* are *greenish or greyish below*.

Gael: Cluas Cait (as English)

OTHER SPECIES: Smooth Cat's-ear (*H. glabra*), with *hairless leaves* and *heads less than 1.5 cm across* is rare in NE Scotland.

Autumn Hawkbit

Leontodon autumnalis
DAISY FAMILY

Autumn Hawkbit is distinguished from Dandelions by its *slender, branched stems, which lack milky juice* and from Cat's-ear by its *shiny hairless leaves* and the *absence of scales between its florets*. Its stems stand to 50 cm tall, and are only *slightly swollen*, with *numerous scale-like bracts* below the flowerheads. These are 1.5-3.5 cm across, with a *woolly* cup of *bracts* at their base and with *outer ray-florets* which are *reddish below*. The plant grows in pastures and waysides throughout Scotland.

Gael: Caisearbhan Coitcheann (origin obscure; may contain cas = 'foot', searbhan = 'bitter one'; coitcheann = 'common')

OTHER SPECIES: Rough Hawkbit (*L. hispidus*), with *leaves covered in forked hairs* and *larger flowerheads*, grows in lime-rich grassland in the S.

Nipplewort

Lapsana communis
DAISY FAMILY

This slender annual is distinguished from other all dandelion-like plants by its *fruits*, which *lack a parachute of hairs*. Its *leafy, branched stems* are *hairy at the base* and 15-125 cm tall. Its *lower leaves* are *lobed*, with the *lobe at the tip much the largest*; the upper stem leaves are less divided and stalkless. It flowers in summer and autumn, with *long-stalked flowerheads*, about 2 cm across, in a *branching inflorescence*. It grows in waysides and hedgerows around Scotland, but less commonly in the NW and Isles.

Gael: Duilleag-bhràghad ('Breast-leaf')

Smooth Hawksbeard

Crepis capillaris
DAISY FAMILY

The *wiry, branching stems* of this annual are up to 90 cm tall, *hairy at the base* with *few stem leaves* which are *lance-shaped, lobed or toothed*, and *never densely hairy*. The upper leaves have a *clasping, arrow-shaped base*. The flowerheads, in an *open, branching inflorescence* in summer, are *1-2 cm across* with a *double row of bracts* at their base. The outer florets are often *reddish underneath*. The plant grows in grassland, heaths and wasteground around Scotland, but rarely far inland.

Gael: Lus Curain Mìn ('Smooth Foam Plant')

OTHER SPECIES: Marsh Hawksbeard (*C. paludosa*), with *hairless leaves and stems* and *woolly bracts*, is widespread in wet places.

Mouse-eared Hawkweed

Pilosella officinarum
DAISY FAMILY

Hawkweeds (*Hieracium* and *Pilosella* species) are a large group of many 'microspecies'. All are perennials with *hairy stems, hairy leaves* which are generally *oblong, unlobed and only slightly toothed*, and yellow or orange-red dandelion-like flowers in summer. Some have leaves up the stem, but Mouse-eared Hawkweed *has only rosette leaves*, which are *white-felted beneath*. Its *stem is unbranched and leafless* with a *solitary flowerhead*. It grows in grassland throughout Scotland.

Gael: Srubhan na Muice ('Pig's Snout')

94

Common Twayblade

Listera ovata
ORCHID FAMILY

Easily overlooked despite its sturdy, *hairy stems* to 60 cm tall, this orchid grows in base-rich grassland, open woodland and dunes in the S and near coasts in the N and Isles. It has a *single pair* of broadly oval, *ribbed leaves, 5-20 cm long*. In midsummer, it produces a *loose spike* of *yellowish-green flowers*, with *hooded upper lobes*, 2 side lobes like arms, and a *long, deeply forked lower lip*. (cf Lesser Twayblade, p. 208).

Gael: *Dà-dhuilleach* ('Two-leaved' (Plant))

Greater Butterfly Orchid

Platanthera chlorantha
ORCHID FAMILY

This handsome orchid, 20-40 cm tall, usually has a *single pair* of oblong *basal leaves* and a few smaller stem leaves. In early summer, it has a *loose, pyramidal spike* of greenish-white, *vanilla-scented flowers*, with 3 spreading upper lobes, and a *strap-shaped* lower lip. The *down-curved spur* behind the flower is *19-28 mm long*, and the yellow *pollen-sacs* in the flower's mouth *form an inverted V*. It is uncommon in woods and lime-rich grassland, mostly in the W.

Gael: *Mogairlean an Dealain-dè Mòr* ('Large Butterfly Orchid')

OTHER SPECIES: The slightly shorter Lesser Butterfly Orchid (*P. bifolia*), with *an almost horizontal spur less than 20 mm long*, and *parallel pollen-sacs*, grows in poorer soils over a similar range.

95

Small White Orchid

Pseudorchis albida
ORCHID FAMILY

More attractive than its prosaic common name might suggest, this is a slender plant, 10-30 cm tall. Its few lower *leaves* are *oblong*, glossy and *folded like a boat keel*, while its 1 or 2 upper stem leaves are *smaller and bract-like*. In midsummer it produces a *dense, cylindrical spike* of *greenish white, bell-shaped flowers*. These are *strongly hooded*, with a *short, 3-lobed* lower lip, about 2 mm long, and a *stumpy, down-curved spur*. The plant grows in rough hill pastures and open moorland in the NW and, more rarely, in the Borders.

Gael: *Mogairlean Bàn Beag (as English; Mogairlean - see p. 206)*

Fragrant Orchid

Gymnadenia conopsea
ORCHID FAMILY

A showy species of lime-rich grassland, fens and marshes throughout the Scottish uplands, Fragrant Orchid even grows on roadside banks in the NW. It stands to 40 cm tall, with a few, *narrow, folded leaves* and a *dense, cylindrical spike* in summer of *rosy-pink to whitish flowers* which are *covered in glistening scales* and *smell richly of carnations*. The flowers are *strongly hooded*, their bottom lips are divided into 3, more or less equally-sized *rounded lobes*, and their *slender, down-curved spurs* are *about 12 mm long*.

Gael: *Lus Taghte ('Chosen/Select Plant')*

Hybrids between the above 2 species, intermediate in form, are sometimes found in the NW.

Common Spotted Orchid

Dactylorhiza fuchsii
ORCHID FAMILY

One of the purple orchid group (p. 206), this is less common than its moorland relatives, with different forms in lime-rich grassland in the S and in machair and limestone rocks in the W. It is 15-70 cm tall, with 5-12, *keeled, dark-blotched leaves*. The *flowers*, borne in dense, cylindrical spikes in midsummer, are pale pink with *red spots and dashes*. These resemble other purple orchids, but with the lower lip *divided into 3 triangular lobes, the middle of which is longest*.

Gael: Urach-bhallach (perhaps 'Spotted Bottle Orchid')
This species often hybridises confusingly with other purple orchids.

Early Purple Orchid

Orchis mascula
ORCHID FAMILY

This *spring-flowered* orchid has a basal rosette of *blunt, broad, oblong leaves*, marked with *round, blackish blotches*. The stout stem, to 60 cm tall, with a *few sheathing leaves*, is topped by a loose spike of *purple flowers, often smelling of tom cats*. The *spreading* upper flower-lobes and the lower lip are *folded back*, giving the flowers a squashed appearance. The lip is *about as broad as long*, with 3 *shallow, wavy-edged lobes* and is *paler in the middle with purple spots*. The plant grows in grassland, mountain ledges and open woodland, often with Wild Hyacinth, scattered around Scotland, especially in the W.

Gael: Moth-ùrach (perhaps 'Male Orchid'; ùrach = bottle)

97

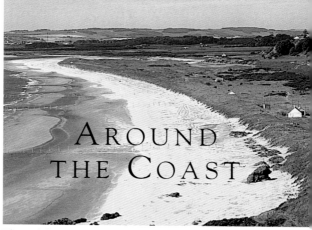

AROUND THE COAST

The sand-dunes and cliffs of St Cyrus in Angus support an interesting flora, including several species at the north of their range

The Scottish mainland has around 3,910 kilometres of coastline, and the many islands add a further 6,290 kilometres. This constitutes two-thirds of the total UK coastline, so it is not surprising that Scotland has a rich variety of seaside flowers. The scenic attractions of rugged cliffs, sweeping beaches, and fiord-like sea-lochs all add greatly to the pleasures of botanising around the shores.

The sea affects plants growing near the coast in three main ways: it warms the land, exposes the coasts to winds and salt-spray, and even floods over saltmarsh plants at the highest tides.

The warming influence of the sea on neighbouring land allows many cold-sensitive species to survive near the coastal strip. As a result, many flowers that are widespread in southern England become confined to coastal regions in Scotland. Scarlet Pimpernel, for example, is an uncommon plant rarely found far from the sea in Scotland, although it is a widespread weed in the south. Plants of sunny

English chalkdowns, such as Carline Thistle and Clustered Bellflower (see p. 238) have just a scattering of sites on sheltered grassy banks in Scotland. The Bellflower, together with two attractive southern limestone plants, Maiden Pink (p. 67) and Nottingham Catchfly (*Silene nutans*), all reach their northernmost British site at St. Cyrus on the Angus coast.

The sand-dune form of the Early Marsh Orchid (p. 207) is called subspecies coccinea from its rich, cochineal-red flowers

Sand-dune systems are often particularly rich in flowers because their hummocks and hollows provide the shelter and sunny banks that encourage both flowers and pollinating insects, while the crushed shells in the sand produce calcium-rich soils in which many species flourish. Many grassland species flower here, along with more typical coastal plants such as Common Storksbill, Spring Vetch and Centaury. The damp hollows between the dunes support a variety of wetland plants, including Water Mint (p. 174), Grass-of-Parnassus (p. 161) and a bewildering array of marsh orchids and their hybrids (p. 206).

The relationship between plants and dunes is even more intimate, because it is plants which encourage the dunes to form. On the seaward side of dune systems, rapidly colonising plants like Sea Rocket and Sand Couch-grass (*Elytrigia juncea*) trap wind-blown sand on the upper beach, allowing low hillocks to form. On these hummocks Marram Grass can establish, just beyond the reach of the tides. Its broad leaves, which roll up into a tube in dry weather to reduce water-loss, act as an efficient trap for more sand. Marram has an extraordinary ability to grow rapidly upwards through the accumulating sand, until huge sand-hills develop. If more sand builds up in the wind than is washed away in storms, sand-dunes can grow progressively out to sea by this process of sand accretion.

The balance between the growth of dunes and their natural attrition by storms is easily disrupted by too many visitors' feet, and erosion is a problem at many popular beaches. It has often been counteracted by planting Lyme Grass, which resembles Marram but has bluish-grey leaves, or the shrubby, orange-berried Sea-buckthorn (*Hippophae rhamnoides*), whose sharp spines

Sea-buckthorn (Hippophae rhamnoides) is sometimes planted to help stabilise eroded sand-dunes. Its orange berries are eaten in the winter by thrushes

act as a living barbed-wire fence guiding visitors away from sensitive areas.

The influence of the sea is not always so benign. Many Scottish coasts, especially in the west and north, are highly exposed, and strong winds and salt spray produce low, windswept grassland, in which only a few resilient plants like Spring Squill and Knotted Pearlwort can flower. In Caithness, Sutherland and Orkney, this clifftop grassland is the home of the rare Scots Primrose, the only instantly-recognisable Scottish endemic flower (that is, one found nowhere else in the world). Where the soil is poorer, especially in the north, the grass is replaced by maritime heathland, often dominated by Crowberry (p. 201), while more southern cliffs are often coloured yellow by the flowers of Whin (p. 193). All too often, these heaths and clifftop grasslands have been ploughed almost to the cliff-edge, virtually destroying the wild coastal ribbon.

Plants of the cliffs include Sea Pink, Sea Campion, Roseroot (a mountain plant which also grows perched on exposed northern sea-cliffs), and Scots Lovage.

Tree Mallow (Lavatera arborea) grows on the Bass Rock and other East Lothian cliff sites and on Ailsa Craig in the Clyde. It was probably introduced by early monks or lighthouse keepers for use in poultices and ointments and to heal burns

101

The name *Scots* Lovage is well-chosen, because it reaches no further south than the Mull of Galloway in the west and just over the English border to Lindisfarne in the east.

Scotland has few sheltered shingle beaches, but where plants have colonised shingle, especially in the north, it is worth searching for Oysterplant, which leads a precarious existence, often disappearing from one site for many years after storms.

Perhaps the least visited of coastal habitats are saltmarshes. These form in sheltered estuaries and bays, where accumulated mud allows colonisation by a range of resistant plants, which are regularly inundated by the sea at the highest tides. Here, according to the poet George Crabbe, 'a grave flora scarcely deigns to bloom', yet in high summer saltmarshes have much to offer the visitor prepared to don wellingtons and carefully check the tides, including colourful banks of Sea Aster along tidal creeks, bright clumps of Thrift and tufts of Sea Plantain and Sea Arrow-grass amongst saltmarsh

Sea Mayweed
(Tripleurospermum
maritimum), *a close
relative of the Scentless
Mayweed of fields
(p. 60), grows on rocks
and shingle near the sea.
Photo by Sue Scott*

Saltmarshes support a range of highly adapted plants, such as the Sea Aster growing along this tidal creek on the Firth of Forth

grasses, delicate Sea Milkwort flowers, and strange, cactus-like Glassworts on open, muddy shores. Most have waxy leaves to repel seawater, and many are fleshy to store freshwater in the fast-draining mud.

Beyond the saltmarsh, the Eelgrasses are the only truly marine Scottish flowering plants, growing and flowering up to 4 metres below the lowest tides.

Thrift or Sea-pink produces glorious displays of colour on rocky shores in early summer

103

Common Scurvy-grass

Cochlearia officinalis
CABBAGE FAMILY

Scurvy-grasses are low-growing, *spring-flowered* plants of cliffs, shingle, saltmarshes and banks round coasts. They have crucifer flowers (p. 45), but produce *globular, oval fruits*. Their *fleshy, oval leaves*, rich in Vitamin C, were formerly eaten to prevent scurvy. This species is distinguished by its *heart-shaped basal leaves, stalkless, clasping upper stem leaves*, and *white or mauve flowers, 10-15 mm across*.
Gael: Am Maraiche ('The Sailor')

OTHER SPECIES: Danish Scurvy-grass (C. *danica*) with *ivy-shaped, mostly stalked and not clasping stem leaves* and *pale lilac flowers about 5 mm across*, is less common around E and W coasts. English Scurvy-grass (C. *anglica*), a *more robust plant with white flowers 9-14 mm across*, and *oblong lower leaves tapering into a long stalk*, may occur much more rarely. Two other *less fleshy* species grow in mossy mountain springs.

Knotted Pearlwort

Sagina nodosa
PINK FAMILY

The only common pearlwort with *relatively showy, 5-petalled flowers* in summer, to *1 cm across*, this tufted perennial has wiry stems to 15 cm tall, with *clusters of short, narrow leaves* forming 'knots' up the stem. It grows scattered around Scotland, including the Isles, in clifftop grassland and other damp grassland, mostly near the coast.
Gael: Mungan Snaimte ('Knotted Mungan' - see p. 20)

Sea Campion

Silene uniflora
PINK FAMILY

Often abundant on sea-cliffs, coastal gravels and shingle around Scotland, Sea Campion has numerous *prostrate shoots* forming mats of *waxy, bluish, lance-shaped leaves* to 3 cm long. A few flowering shoots, to 25 cm tall, arise from this, topped in spring and summer by *1-4 (rarely 7) flowers, 20-25 mm across.* These have an *inflated, bladder-like sepal-tube* with a *broad mouth*, and 5 *deeply notched petals* with a *prominent ruff of scales* around the flower's throat.

Gael: *Coirean na Mara ('Little Sea Cauldron')*

OTHER SPECIES: Bladder Campion (*S. vulgaris*) is similar but *not mat-forming*. It has longer *oblong leaves* and branched inflorescences of *5 or more flowers, about 18 mm across*, with *small petal scales* and *inflated but narrow-mouthed sepal-tubes*. It grows on roadside verges and grassland in the S and E (cf White Campion, p. 25).

Kidney Vetch

Anthyllis vulneraria
PEA FAMILY

Kidney-vetch grows on sunny, lime-rich cliffs and banks near the sea and in mountains inland, scattered around Scotland. It is a *silky-haired* perennial with stems to 60 cm tall and leaves to 14 cm long with *3-7 pairs of narrowly oval leaflets*, topped by a broader leaflet. In summer it has *crowded, roundish, usually paired heads* to 4 cm across of *tightly-compressed pea-flowers* (p. 71) with *woolly sepal-tubes* and longer, *yellow or reddish petals*.

Gael: *Cas an Uain ('Lamb's Foot')*

English Stonecrop

Sedum anglicum
STONECROP FAMILY

Stonecrops typically are perennials with fleshy, undivided, hairless leaves and small flowers with 5 petals and sepals. English Stonecrop fits this norm, with *dense mats of fleshy, balloon-like. reddish leaves, about 4 mm long,* produced on *creeping, rooting stems* to 5 cm long. Its starry, early summer *flowers are about 12 mm across* with 5 *white petals tinged pink beneath.* It is common on rocks, dry grassland and sand-dunes in W Scotland, but rarer in the E and N Isles.

Gael: *Biadh an t-Sionaidh ('Food of the Prince')*

OTHER SPECIES: White Stonecrop (*S. album*), with *cylindrical leaves, 6-12 mm long,* and *branched inflorescences* of smaller white flowers, grows on rocks and walls in the E.

Roseroot

Sedum rosea
STONECROP FAMILY

Less typically a Stonecrop, Roseroot grows on coastal and mountain cliffs, especially in the N and W. Its stems, to 30 cm tall, arise from a *fleshy rootstock,* which smells of roses when cut. It has *thick, flat, bluish leaves,* 1-4 cm long, and *rounded* heads of *greenish-yellow, 4-petalled flowers* in summer. The male flowers (with stamens) are 6 mm across, with petals longer than sepals. They grow on *separate plants* from the females, which have petals equalling the sepals and develop into a cluster of *orange pods.*

Gael: *Lus nan Laoch ('The Heroes' Plant')*

106

Scots Lovage

Ligusticum scoticum
CARROT FAMILY

This tufted perennial grows on cliffs, coastal rocks and occasionally on sand-dunes beyond the reach of grazing animals, all round Scotland and the Isles (see p. 102). Its *ribbed, reddish stems* stand to 90 cm tall, with *glossy, hairless leaves* divided in 3 segments which are themselves 3-lobed. The typical carrot flowers (p. 30) in summer are *greenish-white or pinkish*, in heads up to 6 cm across with 8-14 rays, and develop into *egg-shaped fruits with narrow wings*.

Gael: *Sunais (derivation obscure)*
The bitter leaves of this species are sometimes eaten in salads.

Wild Carrot

Daucus carota
CARROT FAMILY

This wild ancestor of the cultivated carrot has whitish roots which do not swell into the familiar orange vegetable. Like garden carrots, it has *ridged, roughly hairy stems* to 1m tall and *rather thick, much-divided, feathery leaves*. In midsummer, it produces dense, *flat-topped inflorescences* of *whitish flowers*, with numerous, *finely-divided bracts* at its base. The inflorescence usually has a *deep purple central flower*, and its *outermost petals are often enlarged*. The flowers develop into *spiny, flattened oval fruits*. Wild Carrot grows on cliffs, dunes and rocky places near the sea in the W and more rarely in the E, with garden escapes occasionally found elsewhere.

Gael: *Curran Fiadhain (as English)*

107

Thrift

Armeria maritima
THRIFT FAMILY

Also known as Sea Pink, this familiar seaside plant flowers abundantly in spring and summer on coastal rocks, pastures and saltmarshes all round Scottish coasts (see p. 103), and also grows, less commonly, on windswept mountain plateaux. Its *narrow, fleshy leaves* form *dense cushions*, from which arise *downy, leafless flowerstalks*, to 30 cm tall. These are topped by a *solitary, hemispherical inflorescence*, surrounded by brown, papery bracts, with numerous, short-stalked, *rosy-pink to white flowers*. The flowers are about 8 mm across, with 5 petals, united at their base, and a funnel-shaped sepal-tube with pointed teeth ending in a bristle.

Gael: *Neòinean Cladaich* ('Shore Daisy')

Scots Primrose

Primula scotica
PRIMROSE FAMILY

This rare Scottish endemic grows, sometimes abundantly within a small area, in windswept clifftop turf at a few sites on the N coast and Orkney (see pp.242 and 244). It has a basal rosette of short, *spoon-shaped leaves* which are pale-green above and *whitish* beneath. Its *leafless, mealy flowerstems* are 2-10 cm tall. It has 2 flowering periods, in May and, more profusely, in July, but its *rich purple, tubular flowers*, about 8 mm across with a *yellow eye*, are surprisingly easily overlooked.

Gael: *Sòbhrach Albannach* ('Scottish Primrose')

Individual plants, although small, have been shown to live for at least 20 years.

Buckshorn Plantain

Plantago coronopus
PLANTAIN FAMILY

Although its cylindrical inflorescence belongs unmistakably to a plantain (see p. 87), this is the only British species with *deeply-lobed leaves*, supposedly resembling deer antlers. The *rather downy* plant, to 6 cm tall, often lies low over the ground, with leafless *flowerstalks curving upwards* from a horizontal base in the middle of the leaf rosette. The *inflorescence* is fertile, with anthers displayed, in early summer, and is *up to 4 cm long*. The plant is common in bare ground and rocks near the sea around Scottish coasts and islands, its rosettes even surviving heavy trampling.

Gael: *Adhairc Fèidh* ('Deer Horn')

Spring Squill

Scilla verna
LILY FAMILY

Sometimes resembling a miniature Wild Hyacinth (p. 149), this attractive perennial is common in coastal grassland and rocks along the N coast and round the N Isles; it is less common in SW Scotland and the W islands, and very occasional on E coasts. Its *thick, glossy, narrow, rather twisted leaves* lie low amongst the grass, and its leafless flowerstalks stand *5-15 cm tall*, topped in spring by short spikes of a few *violet-blue flowers* with *wide-spreading petal lobes*, intermixed with *bluish, lance-shaped bracts*. The flowers pass quickly, but the *shiny, round, black fruits* last into summer.

Gael: *Lear-uinnean* ('Sea Onion')

109

Greater Sea-spurrey

Spergularia media
PINK FAMILY

Sea-spurreys resemble Corn Spurrey (p. 52) but have pink flowers and a *papery collar round the stem* at the base of each leaf-whorl. Greater Sea-spurrey is a *hairless perennial*, with *pale pink or whitish petals, a little longer* than the sepals, in *flowers 8-12 mm across*. A final check is to open a fruit and examine with a lens the *seeds*, which have *broad wings*. It grows in scattered saltmarshes around the coast and islands.

Gael: *Corran Mara Mòr ('Large Sea Spurrey'* - see p. 52)

OTHER SPECIES: Lesser Sea-spurrey (*S. marina*), an *annual* with *flowers 6-8 mm across*, petals *shorter* than sepals and mostly *unwinged seeds*, is less common in saltmarshes. Rock Sea-spurrey (*S. rupicola*) with *glandular-hairy leaves* and *deep pink petals* longer than the sepals, grows on sea-cliffs in the SW (p. 230), and Sand Spurrey (*S. rubra*) with *long-pointed leaves* and *rosy flowers, 3-5 mm across*, grows in sandy soils inland.

Sea Plantain

Plantago maritima
PLANTAIN FAMILY

This typical plantain has *tight rosettes* of *narrow, fleshy leaves* and *cylindrical flowerheads* with *conspicuous pale-yellow stamens* in summer. It has *thicker, narrower, less strongly-veined leaves* than Ribwort Plantain (p. 87), and its *flowerstalks lack grooves*. It grows in saltmarshes and coastal turf around Scotland and also beside mountain streams.

Gael: *Slàn-lus na Mara ('Healing Plant of the Sea')*

Annual Seablite

Sueda maritima
GOOSEFOOT FAMILY

A very variable annual of saltmarshes and sea-shores, Annual Seablite grows scattered round Scottish coasts, usually below the high tide mark and often with Glasswort (below). It has red-tinged, *sprawling stems* to 30 cm long, and *fleshy, pointed, half-cylindrical leaves*, 3-25 mm long. Its *tiny, greenish flowers*, with *2 minute bracteoles*, develop in late summer, singly or in clumps of 2 or 3, *in the angles of the upper leaves*. The flowers have 5 fleshy lobes and are either female without stamens, or hermaphrodite with 5 stamens.

Gael: Praiseach na Mara ('Sea Pot One')

Glasswort

Salicornia europaea
GOOSEFOOT FAMILY

Scottish glassworts are a group of similar annuals, separated on details of their inflorescences and branching, but all sharing an *erect, succulent, cactus-like form*. Their *branching, cylindrical stems* are 10-40 cm tall, with paired leaves fused into *fleshy sheaths* around the stem. Their minute *petal-less flowers* develop in late summer, with just their 1 or 2 stamens obvious. They grow above each sheath near branch ends, in *triangular groups of 3* sunk into the stem (see illustration). Glassworts grow on open mud near the low tide mark of saltmarshes, scattered around Scottish coasts, particularly in the S and W. Their burnt ash was once used to make glass.

Gael: Lus na Glainne ('Glass Plant')

Sea Aster

Aster tripolium
DAISY FAMILY

Reminiscent of (and closely related to) garden Michaelmas Daisies, Sea Aster is a *hairless perennial* with sturdy stems, 15-100 cm tall, and *fleshy, lance-shaped, only slightly toothed leaves*. It flowers in late summer, producing showy daisy flowers (p. 60), to 2 cm across, with *yellow disc florets* and spreading *blue-purple or pale lilac rays*. (A rayless variety, with yellow button flowers is very rare in Scotland). Sea Aster is confined mainly to sheltered estuaries and inlets in Scotland, especially alongside muddy channels (see p. 103), but it also grows on salt-sprayed sea-cliffs and rocks, especially in the N.
Gael: Neòinean Sàilein ('Sea-inlet Daisy')

Sea Arrowgrass

Triglochin maritimum
ARROWGRASS FAMILY

This inconspicuous perennial of saltmarshes and salt-sprayed turf all round the coast and islands has leafless stems, 15-60 cm tall, and a basal tuft of *long, half-cylindrical, fleshy leaves* (more upright and grass-like than those of Sea Plantain, p. 110). In summer, it produces *dense spikes* of *tiny flowers (top detail)*, with 6 green lobes and a tufted white style. They ripen into *egg-shaped fruits*, about 4 mm long (lower detail).
Gael: Bàrr a' Mhilltich Mara ('Sea Top of the Grassy Tufts')

OTHER SPECIES: Marsh Arrowgrass (*T. palustris*), with *less fleshy leaves, densely furrowed near their base*, and *arrow-shaped fruits* about 8 mm long, grows in upland marshes, usually amongst tall grass.

Sea Milkwort

Glaux maritima
PRIMROSE FAMILY

This *rather fleshy, hairless* perennial with *oblong leaves* creeps amongst other vegetation in the upper zone of saltmarshes or in salt-sprayed turf and rock crevices, round Scottish coasts and islands. Its *stalkless flowers* appear in summer in the angles of the upper leaves. They lack petals, but have a *delicate pink to white sepal-tube, 3-5 mm in diameter,* with 5 *rounded lobes.*
Gael: *Lus na Sailleachd ('Plant of the Saltiness')*

Eelgrass

Zostera marina
EELGRASS FAMILY

Eelgrass leaves are often washed up on shores, but the plant grows submerged to depths of 4m below low water on muddy and sandy seabeds and in brackish lagoons. It is widespread round W coasts and islands, but uncommon and declining in E coast estuaries. Its *grass-like leaves* are 20-200 cm long and 5-10 mm wide, with *pointed tips.* Its *minute flowers* develop in summer in *2 rows, partly enclosed in sheaths,* towards the base of leaf-like branches (see illustration).
Gael: *Bilearach (possibly from bile = lip or edge)*

OTHER SPECIES: Narrow-leaved Eelgrass (*Z. angustifolia*), with *round-tipped leaves about 2 mm wide,* grows in shallow water, mainly around the Solway, Forth and Moray Firths. Dwarf Eelgrass (*Z. noltii*), with *leaves under 1 mm wide* with *notched tips,* grows higher on the shore by muddy creeks, over a similar range but including the Argyll coast.

113

Babington's Orache

Atriplex glabriuscula
GOOSEFOOT FAMILY

The commonest Orache growing above the high-tide mark on sandy or gravelly shores round Scottish coasts, this is a sprawling, *mealy* annual, with *stems to 20 cm long*, often *striped white or red and green*. It has *thick, triangular, shallowly toothed leaves* and *slender, open, leafy spikes* of *tiny, greenish, unstalked flowers*. The male and female flowers are separate on the same plant, the females developing into fruits enclosed by *2 warty, diamond-shaped bracts*.

Gael: *Praiseach-mhìn Chladaich* ('Smooth Broth of the Shore')

OTHER SPECIES: Five similar species, distinguished by leaf and bracteole shape, grow less commonly on Scottish coasts. Common Orache (*A. patula*), with sprawling *stems to 1m long* and *mealy, diamond-shaped leaves*, is a common lowland weed of cultivated ground.

Oysterplant

Mertensia maritima
BORAGE FAMILY

Least rare on the N Isles, this distinctive plant of stony shores is declining in the S and scarce and highly mobile everywhere. It forms *bluish patches* on the shore, with sprawling stems, (less erect than shown; see p. 231) to 60 cm long and opposite rows of *fleshy, oval, blue-washed leaves*. Its *tubular flowers*, produced in midsummer in short, branched, leafy inflorescences, are about 6 mm *across* and *open pink then turn blue*.

Gael: *Tiodhlac na Mara* ('Gift of the Sea')

Sea Rocket

Cakile maritima
CABBAGE FAMILY

A common plant of the strandline on sandy and shingly shores round most of Scotland and the islands, Sea Rocket traps sand on the seaward edge of sand-dunes, forming low foredunes. Its long tap-root produces patches of straggling stems to 45 cm long, with *fleshy, deeply-lobed, oblong leaves* which *narrow into a stalk-like base*. In summer, the stems and branches end in dense inflorescences of *mauve to white flowers*, about 15 mm across. These have 4 petals, twice as long as the sepals, and ripen into stubby, *2-jointed fruit pods*, 10-25 mm long, which are dispersed by the tide.

Gael: *Fearsaideag ('Little Estuary One')*

Prickly Saltwort

Salsola kali
GOOSEFOOT FAMILY

Another salt-tolerant member of the Goosefoot family, Prickly Saltwort grows on sandy shores, with a scattered distribution around E and W coasts and islands, but is probably now gone from the N Isles. It is a *much-branched, sprawling, grey-green* annual to 60 cm long with stalkless, *short, fat, fleshy leaves*, ending in a *sharp spiny tip*. Its inconspicuous, greenish flowers appear in late summer in the angles of upper leaves, protected by *2 prickly bracteoles*. The 5 flower lobes then toughen to enclose the *top-shaped fruit*.

Gael: *Lus an t-Salainn ('Salt Plant')*
The burnt ash of Saltwort was once used to make washing soda.

115

Lesser Meadow-rue

Thalictrum minus
BUTTERCUP FAMILY

This easily overlooked perennial has *wiry, wavy, branching stems*, 15-40 cm tall (taller at inland sites), with *leaves* divided into *many wedge-shaped lobes*. In summer, it has a *spreading, much-branched inflorescence*, drooping at first and later erect, of insignificant *flowers with 4, greenish-yellow lobes* and a *hanging tassel of yellow stamens*. It is very variable, the commonest form growing in sand-dunes round the coast except for the SW and Shetland, with a larger form on lime-rich rocks in the S Highlands. (cf Alpine Meadow-rue, p. 218).

Gael: Rù Beag ('Small Rue')

OTHER SPECIES: Common Meadow-rue (*T. flavum*), to *1 m tall* with a *narrow end leaf segment* and a *dense head* of flowers with *upright stamens*, grows in a few lowland meadows.

Sea Sandwort

Honckenya peploides
PINK FAMILY

The leafy shoots of this *succulent* perennial form *dense patches* on sandy or shingly foreshores all round Scotland, as well as in W Isles machair. Its *stiff, yellow-green, pointed oval leaves* are *densely ranked* up the stems, which are 5-25 cm tall. In spring and summer, it produces many *greenish-white flowers*, less than 1 cm across, with *5 narrow petals* as long as the sepals in male flowers and much shorter in female flowers which are often on separate plants.

Gael: Lus a' Ghoill ('Foreigner's/Stranger's Plant')

Common Storksbill

Erodium cicutarium
GERANIUM FAMILY

Closely related to Cranesbills (p. 26), Storksbills have fruits with an *even longer beak* (to 4 cm long). Common Storksbill, the only Scottish species, has a basal rosette of *feathery leaves*, 2-20 cm long, *with many, deeply-cut lobes*, and stout, rather hairy stems to 60 cm tall. It flowers in summer, producing *umbrella-like groups* of up to 9 flowers, about 12 mm across, with *rosy-pink, rounded petals*, 2 of which may be dark-spotted. It grows in dune grassland and sandy fields inland, commonly in E coastal areas, more rarely on the W coast and islands, and as a rare casual on the N Isles.

Gael: Gob Corra ('Stork's Bill')

Purple Milk-vetch

Astragalus danicus
PEA FAMILY

This creeping perennial is commonest amongst sand-dunes or coastal turf in the SE, but also grows in lime-rich grassland inland in the SE and Perthshire, on clifftops in Galloway, and in hay meadows on Tiree. It has *vetch-like, softly hairy leaves*, 3-7 cm long, with *6-13 pairs* of narrow leaflets, *ending in a leaflet* not a tendril. Its *blue-purple flowers* develop in early summer on leafless, *white-haired stalks*, longer than the leaves, in tight, roundish, *upward-facing clusters* of around 15 flowers. These are about 15 mm long, with a toothed sepal-tube covered in a *mat of black and white hairs*.

Gael: Bliochd-pheasair Chorcarach (as English)

Spring Vetch

Vicia lathyroides
PEA FAMILY

Like a miniature Common Vetch (p. 69) but with smaller flowers, fewer leaflets and *no blotch underneath its leaf appendages*, this slender annual creeps over dune grassland or dry grassy banks, never far from the sea, near E and SW coasts only. Its typical vetch leaves have *2-4 pairs of narrow leaflets*, 4-14 mm long, and end in a *small, unbranched tendril* (often absent). The solitary, *blue-lilac spring flowers* are about 6 mm long, and ripen into a *hairless pod*. The *flowers are longer and darker* than those of Hairy Tare (p. 69), which has more leaflets and hairy pods.

Gael: *Peasair an Earraich* ('Spring Pea')

Burnet Rose

Rosa pimpinellifolia
ROSE FAMILY

Spreading by suckers, this low shrub forms *bushy patches* in dunes, sandy coastal heaths and inland limestone grassland round the mainland coast and W islands, although it is rare on the outer W Isles and absent from the N Isles. Its erect stems, to 40 cm tall, are densely covered in *long, straight prickles*, mixed with *stiff bristles*. Its leaves have *7-11 rounded, toothed lobes*. Its solitary, *creamy-white flowers*, 25-40 mm across, appear in early summer, the sepals remaining as a tuft crowning the *purplish-black hips* (fruits) which then develop.

Gael: *Ròs Beag Bàn na h-Alba* ('Little White Rose of Scotland')

Biting Stonecrop

Sedum acre
STONECROP FAMILY

Resembling English Stonecrop (p. 106), this is distinguished by its early summer *yellow flowers*, about 12 mm across, and its *bright-green* (or occasionally reddish), fleshy, oval *leaves*, 3-5 mm long. If nibbled cautiously, it has a distinctive *peppery taste*, earning it the alternate name of Wall Pepper. Its creeping stems, 2-10 cm long, form succulent mats in sand-dunes, dry grassland, shingle and walls, inland in the S and E and round coasts including the W Isles and Orkney but only where planted on Shetland.

Gael: Grabhan nan Clach (perhaps 'Pick-axe of the Stones')

OTHER SPECIES: Reflexed Stonecrop (*S. rupestre*), a taller plant with *bent-down leaves to 20 mm long* and larger flowers, is a rare garden escape.

Sea Holly

Eryngium maritimum
CARROT FAMILY

The least carrot-like member of its family, Sea Holly has *fleshy, prickly, waxy, bluish-green leaves*, up to 12 cm across, with smaller, more lobed, stalkless stem leaves. The stems stand 15-60 cm tall, topped in midsummer by *egg-shaped heads*, about 2 cm across, of *steely blue flowers*, almost buried amongst spiny bracteoles. A plant of sandy and shingle foreshores, it is apparently now extinct in the E, but grows uncommonly around the Solway and Clyde, and on Coll, Tiree and a few other W islands.

Gael: Cuileann Tràgha ('Shore Holly')

119

Scarlet Pimpernel

Anagallis arvensis
PRIMROSE FAMILY

Much less common than in S Britain, this sprawling annual grows in dunes and light cultivated ground near E and SW coasts, on a few W islands, and as a rare garden weed on the N Isles. It has *weak, square stems* to 30 cm long, with *stalkless, narrowly oval leaves*, dotted with *black glands* underneath. Its slender-stalked flowers, which appear in summer, are 12-15 mm across, with 5 spreading *scarlet or pink petal-lobes* that open only in sunshine and close by early afternoon. A blue-flowered form occurs rarely.

Gael: Falcair (possibly 'Cleanser' from failc = bathe).

OTHER SPECIES: Chaffweed (*A. minima*), a *tiny annual* to 5 cm long with *minute whitish flowers* almost hidden in the angles of its oval leaves, is rare near E and W coasts.

Sea Bindweed

Calystegia soldanella
BINDWEED FAMILY

The main difference between this and other bindweeds (p. 57) is that, rather than twining round other vegetation, its stems *creep through the sand or shingle* of beaches, producing scattered patches of *rather fleshy, glossy, kidney-shaped leaves*. Amongst these, in summer, appear solitary, long-stalked, *funnel-shaped flowers*, 3-5 cm across, with short bracts beneath and petals which are *pink with creamy stripes*. It is restricted to SW coasts, a few W islands, and a solitary E Lothian site.

Gael: Flùr a' Phrionnsa ('The Prince's Flower')

Common Centaury

Centaurium erythraea
GENTIAN FAMILY

This variable biennial has a basal rosette of *elliptical leaves*, 8-12 mm wide, and one or more erect, branching stems, 2-50 cm tall. The branches are topped in summer by a dense, *flat-topped cluster* of *stalkless, pink, tubular flowers*, with 5 spreading petal lobes about 1 cm in diameter. It grows in sand-dunes mostly round SE and W coasts and islands, with a few sites on dry grassland inland.

Gael: Ceud-bhileach ('Hundred-leaved')

OTHER SPECIES: Seaside Centaury (*C. littorale*), with a rosette of *narrow leaves* to 5 mm wide and *few-flowered heads*, grows in coastal turf mostly around the SW and Moray Firth.

Houndstongue

Cynoglossum officinale
BORAGE FAMILY

The name of this sturdy, *mousy-smelling* biennial comes from its *tongue-shaped leaves* which are *grey with a web of silky hairs* on both surfaces. The plant stands to 90 cm tall, with a few stalked basal leaves and many stalkless stem-leaves which cluster round the stem and half enclose the flowers. These appear in tight clusters in summer, and have a *dull maroon* (rarely white) *petal-tube* that is about 1 cm across. They ripen into *fruits with 4 nutlets and covered in barbed spines* which readily attach to clothing or even skin.

Gael: Teanga a' Choin (as English)

121

Henbane

Hyoscyamus niger
NIGHTSHADE FAMILY

Restricted in Scotland mainly to sandy shores, this *foul-smelling* annual or biennial grows scattered along the E and SW coasts, and as a rare casual on Orkney. Its stout stem stands to 80 cm tall and is covered, like its *oblong, broadly-toothed leaves*, in *sticky, white hairs*. In summer its stems are topped by clusters of *urn-shaped, buff yellow flowers, veined with purple*, 2-3 cm across, with 5 petal-lobes. All parts of the plant, including the seeds, are very poisonous.

Gael: Gafann (derivation obscure)

OTHER SPECIES: The even more poisonous Deadly Nightshade (*Atropa bella-donna*), with *bell-shaped, dull purple flowers* and *glossy black berries*, is a rare introduction mostly in the E.

Cornsalad

Valerianella locusta
VALERIAN FAMILY

This *slender, hairless* annual, also known as Lamb's Lettuce, grows most commonly in dune grassland, where its stems are often so short that only the cup of *pale lilac, funnel-shaped flowers*, enclosed by bracts, is visible in *springtime*, the whole plant withering soon after. On walls or rocky outcrops, its brittle, branching stems grow rather taller, to 40 cm high, with *opposite pairs of oblong leaves*. It is found scattered through S Scotland and the W islands, more rarely in the N and not on the N Isles.

Gael: Leiteis an Uain ('Lamb's Lettuce')

Carline Thistle

Carlina vulgaris
DAISY FAMILY

The 'everlasting' apparent flowers of this spiny biennial resemble dried thistle heads, but their *straw-coloured 'rays'*, which spread out in dry weather to 3 cm across, are in fact bracts, with the true florets forming the central disc. The *leaves are deeply-cut and prickly*, those in the 1st year forming a *cottony rosette* which withers before the plant flowers. The *flowering stems are purplish and cottony*, to 60 cm tall, with *hairless, half-clasping leaves*. The plant grows uncommonly in sand-dunes and lime-rich grassland in the E, SW and inner W islands.
Gael: *Cluaran Oir ('Golden Thistle')*

Marram Grass

Ammophila arenaria
GRASS FAMILY

Although grasses are generally excluded from this guide, this *far-creeping* perennial is so prominent in sand-dunes around Scottish coasts (see p. 100) that it cannot be omitted. It stands to 1.2 m tall, with *tough, ribbed, sharp-pointed leaves*, which *roll inwards when dry* and are *greyish-green inside and shiny outside*. The *spike-like flowerheads*, 7-20 cm long, appear *whitish from the silky hairs of the crowded flowers*.

Gael: *Muran (from muir = the sea)*
Muran leaves are traditionally used for thatching in the W Isles.

OTHER SPECIES: Lyme Grass (*Leymus arenarius*), up to 1.5 m tall with *broader, more bluish-grey leaves* and *coarser, spikier flowerheads* grows mainly in E coast dunes, often with Marram.

April is colourful in the woods of Argyll, with Primrose, Lesser Celandine and Common Dog-violet flowering beneath the trees

A lthough the Highlands are traditionally the main attraction for visitors, the Scottish Lowlands also have much to offer. Indeed, anyone in search of wild flowers in springtime will find more colour and variety in lowland woods or along riverbanks than in the Highlands, where the climate stops most plants from flowering until well into May.

Rather few natural woods remain in Scotland. In Argyll there are still some superb areas of oak woodland – at Glen Nant, near Taynuilt (see 'Places to Visit'), or Taynish, south-west of Lochgilphead, for example. Gnarled and twisted by the winds, these woods are just as wild as the pinewoods of the central Highlands, and, in recognition of this, Glen Nant has been declared a Caledonian Forest

Reserve by the Forestry Commission, the government forestry department. Many of these woods were coppiced in the past to produce charcoal for the gunpowder industry in the area. Their main interest botanically is in the lichens and liverworts that carpet their trunks, but the floor beneath the trees is colourful in May and June with woodland flowers including Wood Anemones, Primroses and Wild Hyacinths.

In the central Lowlands, almost the only natural woodland left after past felling clings to the steep banks of river gorges, notably along the Clyde near Lanark and in the valley of the Esk south of Edinburgh. The presence of Dog's Mercury here is said to record a continuous woodland history in the area. Certainly, the plant cannot survive long without tree cover, although it will slowly colonise newly-planted woodland from any remaining copse. Other important remnants of ancient woodland survive near Dalkeith in Midlothian and

Many attractive areas of woodland survive in western Scotland, like this on the shores of Loch Linnhe in Inverness-shire

Hamilton in Lanarkshire, preserved as hunting parks. Thanks to the enlightenment of the late eighteenth and early nineteenth century lairds (landowners), fine planted woodland is now an attractive feature in many parts of the Lowlands. These 'policy' woodlands (from the French for 'managed lands') were laid out to provide an attractive setting for the great houses of the lairds, as cover for game birds, as an investment in timber, and also, undoubtedly, for their scientific and amenity value. Non-native species such as Sycamore and Beech were often included in the planting, and it seems that the ground flora was often enhanced by attractive shrubs and herbs which would provide colour throughout the spring and summer.

As a result, these policy woods often host superb displays of alien plants that are uncommon or absent elsewhere in Britain, including Leopardsbane, Pink Purslane, Pyrenean Valerian, and the winter-flowering White Butterbur – as well as true natives such as Lesser Celandine, Wood Stitchwort, Sanicle and Ramsons.

Attractive flowers can be seen where rivers cut through planted woodlands in the Lowlands, as here at Almondell Country Park in West Lothian

Some of these aliens can confuse the unwary visitor. Few-flowered Leek, for example, which flowers abundantly in May, is omitted from many field guides in which the nearest match is a rare Garlic from

Pick-a-back-plant (Tolmeia menziesii) *is a member of the Saxifrage family from North America which has become established in woods and along rivers in southern Scotland*

Cornwall! It spreads by tiny bulbils beneath its flowers, which break off when the plant is cut or grazed and grow into new plants, producing dense carpets in many lowland woods.

With lack of management in recent decades, many policy woodlands have become inaccessible in parts, but, where rivers and streams cut through them, bankside paths are often kept open by anglers. These allow easy access to see both woodland species and a colourful display of riverside plants, such as Marsh Marigold, Cuckooflower, Water Avens and Comfrey. Walks along the River Tweed near St. Boswells and the Clyde at New Lanark (see 'Places to Visit') are particularly attractive in springtime.

Riverbanks also have their share of aliens, some of which have become so abundant that they displace

127

native species. Indian Balsam, a native of the Himalayas, is widespread along the Water of Leith in Edinburgh or the Clyde at Dalmarnock in Glasgow, spread by waterborne seeds from its explosive fruits to form dense hedges in places. A more pernicious alien is Giant Hogweed from the Caucasus. Victorians

Giant Hogweed is an alien from south-west Asia which has established dense thickets along riverbanks in the lowlands

introduced it into their gardens to celebrate its mammoth size (up to 5 m tall), but it soon escaped, spreading along railways and riverbanks. Today it is abundant along parts of the Rivers Clyde and Kelvin in Glasgow, the Tweed and Teviot in the Borders, and rivers around Edinburgh. Because its sap can sensitise the skin to sunlight, causing severe sunburn, attempts are being made to eradicate it in many areas.

After several decades of neglect and infilling, ponds are again being regarded as an important feature of lowland landscapes, especially on farms, and new ponds are being dug into which the natural flora soon moves, often on the feet of birds. The tiny, floating Duckweeds are usually first to arrive, but soon other species such as Water Starwort, Water Crowfoot, Amphibious Bistort and Pondweeds will follow. Many new ponds are now maturing attractively around the Lowlands, although, in the absence of disturbance by drinking cattle and horses, they will need regular dredging to maintain their diversity.

Many of these wetland species also grow around the edges of the lochs dotted around the Lowlands, but the larger size and greater depth of these water bodies also allows dense patches of of Reeds (*Phragmites australis*) or Bottle Sedge (*Carex rostrata*) to grow out into the open water. Amongst the reeds, in damp woods around the loch edge, and in overgrown marshy areas can be found plants like Meadowsweet, Purple Loosestrife, Cowbane, Hemlock and Hemlock Water-dropwort, as well as Yellow Loosestrife and rarer relatives such as Tufted Loosestrife.

Blood-drop-emlets (Mimulus luteus) is one of several cultivated species and hybrids of Monkeyflower which have escaped and now grow on riverbanks and in ditches around Scotland

Wood Anemone

Anemone nemorosa
BUTTERCUP FAMILY

In spring, Wood Anemone carpets deciduous woods and hedgerows throughout Scotland, except for the N coast and W Isles and only as a rare introduction in N Isles plantations. It has 3, *deeply-lobed stem leaves* in a whorl beneath its flowerhead, and similar basal leaves which develop from a far-creeping underground stem after flowering and persist into summer when the flowers have withered. The stem stands to 30 cm tall, with a *single nodding flower*, 2-4 cm across, with *usually 6 or 7 (but up to 12) white or pink-tinged, petal-like lobes.*
Gael: *Flùr na Gaoithe ('Wind Flower')*
The slender-stalked flowers shake in the wind, hence Anemone (from anemos, the Greek for wind) and the alternative name 'Windflower'.

Goldilocks Buttercup

Ranunculus auricomus
BUTTERCUP FAMILY

Flowering in late spring, this uncommon buttercup of nutrient-rich deciduous woodlands in S Scotland and the C Highlands is *less hairy* and *fewer flowered* than Meadow Buttercup (p.42). It has *hairless, kidney-shaped, toothed or shallowly lobed lower leaves* and *few stem leaves* deeply divided into *narrow segments*. Its flowers, to 1 cm across, have *5 or fewer petals* which are soon shed (*or are sometimes absent*), and *5 spreading sepals* which are often *purple-tipped* or yellow in flowers without petals.
Gael: *Gruag Moire ('Mary's Locks')*

Lesser Celandine

Ranunculus ficaria
BUTTERCUP FAMILY

A characteristic spring flower of damp woodland, hedgerows and grassy banks throughout Scotland, apart from the wilder parts of the Highlands and NW, Lesser Celandine can flower from January in the mild SW. It has *long-stalked, glossy, heart-shaped leaves* and *single flowers*, up to 3 cm across, with *8-12 narrow, glossy, yellow petals* and *3 sepals which are shed early*. A straggly form, with white bulbils at the base of its leaf stalks after flowering, is a troublesome weed of disturbed ground and gardens.

Gael: *Searragaich (perhaps from Searrag = a bottle)*

Tutsan

Hypericum androsaemum
ST. JOHN'S-WORT FAMILY

This *semi-evergreen, low-growing shrub (to 1 m tall)* grows in damp woods and hedgerows in the far W, from Argyll to Ross-shire and the inner islands, with a few introductions elsewhere. It has *a stem with 2 raised lines* and many *large, unstalked, oval leaves*. Its *flowers*, which grow in *small clusters* in summer, are *about 2 cm across*, with *5 blunt petals* which are soon shed and *5 unequally-sized sepals*. The flowers develop into berries, which ripen green, red and then purplish-black and can persist into January.

Gael: *Meas an Tuirc-Coille ('Fruit of the Wood Boar')*

OTHER SPECIES: Rose-of-Sharon (*H. calycinum*), an evergreen shrub with *flowers to 8 cm across*, is an occasional introduction, mostly in the SE.

Greater Stitchwort

Stellaria holostea
PINK FAMILY

Stitchworts are rather fragile herbs with narrow leaves in opposite pairs up their slender stems and *starry white flowers with 5 sepals, 5 notched petals and 10 stamens*. They were once used to treat pains in the side ('stitches'). This species grows in woods and hedgerows on the mainland and inner islands, but not the W and N Isles. It stands to 60 cm tall with a *squarish, rough-angled stem* and *stiff, narrow, bluish, rough-edged leaves*, 4-8 cm long, which *taper to a long, fine point*. Its *flowers*, in spring and early summer, are *15-30 mm across*, with *petals longer than the sepals* and *notched to about half-way down*. Beneath the flowers are *green, leaf-like bracts*.
Gael: Tùrsach ('Dejected')

Lesser Stitchwort

Stellaria graminea
PINK FAMILY

Weaker and slenderer than the species above, Lesser Stitchwort has *greener leaves, smooth at the margins* and *without a drawn-out point*, *smoothly 4-angled stems* and *smaller flowers (to 12 mm across)*, developing later in summer. These have *more deeply divided petals* which are *just longer than the 3-veined sepals*, and *thin, papery bracts*. The plant is even more widespread on the mainland than Greater Stitchwort, growing from woods into open heathland and grassland, and occurs uncommonly on the Isles, although introduced on Shetland.
Gael: Tursarain (perhaps 'Dejected One')

Wood Stitchwort

Stellaria nemorum
PINK FAMILY

Less common than the preceding 2 species, Wood Stitchwort grows in damp woods and shady streamsides in the lowlands but not the Highlands or islands. It resembles a tall Common Chickweed (p. 51), with *scrambling stems which are rounded and hairy* and up to 60 cm long. It has *broadly oval leaves* ending in a *short point*, and loose heads, in early summer, of flowers which are 10-18 mm across with *petals divided almost to the base* and *about twice as long as the sepals*.

Gael: *Tursarain Coille* (perhaps 'Dejected One of the Wood')

OTHER SPECIES: Greater Chickweed (*S. neglecta*), a *sprawling plant to 90 cm high* with *flowers to 10 mm across* and *petals just longer than the sepals*, grows in a few scattered hedgerows.

Three-nerved Sandwort

Moehringia trinervia
PINK FAMILY

Found in rich woodland soils throughout the lowlands, Jura and Islay only, this *straggling and easily overlooked annual* resembles Common Chickweed (p. 51) but has a stem that is *downy all round* and *egg-shaped leaves which are strongly 3-5 veined underneath*. Its inconspicuous flowers appear in early summer. They are about 6 mm across, with *undivided petals. about half as long as the narrow sepals* which have *broad white margins*.

Gael: *Lus nan Naoi Alt Trì-Fèitheach* ('3-nerved Plant of the 9 Joints')

133

Pink Purslane

Claytonia sibirica
BLINKS FAMILY

Brought to Britain around 1838 from Pacific N America, this hairless plant, to 40 cm tall, is now surprisingly common in damp woodland through S, C and E Scotland, even growing in plantations on Orkney and Lewis. It has *long-stalked, rather fleshy basal leaves* and *a single pair of equally fleshy, stalkless stem leaves*. Its flowers, in a branching inflorescence in spring and early summer, are *15-20 mm across* with *2 sepals* and *5, much longer, deeply notched, pink or white petals, with darker pink veins*.
Gael: Seachranaiche ('Wanderer' or 'Stranger')

Spring Beauty

Claytonia perfoliata
BLINKS FAMILY

The *fleshy leaves* of this slightly shorter, pale-green annual show its relationship to Pink Purslane (above). The *lower leaves are broadly diamond-shaped and long-stalked*, but the *single pair of stalkless stem leaves are widely joined at their base* forming a ruff around the stem beneath a small group of *white flowers* in early summer. These are *5-8 mm across*, with *5 unnotched petals slightly longer than the 2 sepals*. Originally also from the American Pacific coast, Spring Beauty was introduced to Britain around 1852, and now grows in poor sandy soils at a few sites in E and SW Scotland.
Gael: Lus Toll Putain ('Buttonhole Plant')

134

Wood Sorrel

Oxalis acetosella
WOOD-SORREL FAMILY

This delicate perennial forms pockets of shining flowers in spring on woodland floors or amongst shady rocks to altitudes of 1200 m in the mountains. Its creeping underground stems produce open patches of leaves *with 3, bright-green, wedge-shaped, slightly hairy leaflets*, which *fold up* like a closed umbrella when not in sunshine. The *solitary flowers*, on stalks to 15 cm long, are about 1 cm across with *5 white or lilac petals*, *veined with deeper lilac*. It is found throughout Scotland, although rare in the N Isles.

Gael: *Feada-coille ('Candle of the Wood')*

Wood Avens

Geum urbanum
ROSE FAMILY

Also known as Herb Bennet, this *hairy perennial* has *stems* to 60 cm tall, *arising from a basal rosette of leaves with 2-3 pairs of toothed leaflets and a much larger, rounded end leaflet*. The stem leaves are similar but with fewer leaflets. The *flowers, facing upwards* on long stalks in summer, are 8-15 mm across, with *5 spreading yellow petals* as long as the *narrow green sepals*. It grows in woods and shady places in all but mountainous areas, but is a rare introduction in the W and N Isles.

Gael: *Machall Coille (perhaps 'Large-headed Plant of the Wood')*
Where Wood and Water Avens (p. 160) meet, they commonly hybridise, producing flowers intermediate in colour and shape.

Wild Strawberry

Fragaria vesca
ROSE FAMILY

Like Garden Strawberry (which occasionally grows as an escape in the Lowlands), this leafy perennial spreads by *rooting runners*, but its 'berries' (strictly the swollen flower-base, with the 'pips' as the true fruits) are smaller and sweeter. Its leaves have *3 toothed leaflets* which are *1-6 cm long* and *bright green above, with pale silky hairs flattened against the underside*. Its flowers, in spring and early summer, are about 15 mm across, with *5 broad, overlapping white petals*, on short *hairy stalks*. It grows in open woods and lime-rich grassland over most of Scotland except parts of the Highlands, but is rare in the N Isles.
Gael: Sùbh-làir Fiadhain ('Wild Ground-fruit')

Barren Strawberry

Potentilla sterilis
ROSE FAMILY

Barren Strawberry resembles the previous species, but its fruit is a dry, inedible capsule. Its *runners*, if produced, are *short and non-rooting*. It has similar leaves, but the leaflets are *0.5-2.5 cm long*, with *spreading hairs on the underside* and *end in a tooth much smaller than its neighbours*. The slightly smaller flowers have *narrow, widely-spaced petals*, with the green sepals showing between them. It flowers from early spring in scrub and open woodland but much less commonly in the N and islands.
Gael: Sùbh-làir Brèige ('False Strawberry' – see above)

Common Enchanter's Nightshade

Circaea lutetiana
WILLOWHERB FAMILY

This perennial of shady woodland, *20-60 cm tall*, has *oval, toothed, stiffly hairy leaves* and an open spike in summer of *flowers, 4-7 mm across*, with *2 deeply-notched white petals* and *2 pale green sepals*. Its *club-shaped fruiting capsules* are covered in *white hooked bristles*. It is widespread in the S and SW islands, but rare in the N.

Gael: Fuinseagach (perhaps 'Enchantress's Weed')

OTHER SPECIES: Alpine Enchanter's Nightshade (*C. alpina*), a smaller plant with *hairless leaves* and *dense flower spikes*, is a rare post-glacial relict recorded from Arran and Inverness-shire. Their sterile hybrid (*C. x intermedia*) is the commonest Enchanter's Nightshade in woods and rocky places in the N, but less common in the S. It is *10-45 cm tall* with *sparsely-hairy, toothed, heart-shaped leaves*.

Ivy

Hedera helix
IVY FAMILY

The woody stems of Ivy form carpets on woodland floors or climb to 30 m in trees, hedges or rocks, attached by stem rootlets. Its *dark-green, hairless leaves* have *3 or 5 spreading lobes*, but its upper stem leaves are diamond-shaped and unlobed. In late autumn, it produces *umbrella-like clusters of greenish-yellow, 5-petalled flowers*, about 5 mm across, which develop into *black berries*. It is found almost throughout Scotland.

Gael: Eidheann (name possibly associated with 'holding on')

Sanicle

Sanicula europaea
CARROT FAMILY

Characteristically growing in dappled sunlight on the floor of deciduous woods, this *hairless* perennial has thin, *long-stalked, rounded, glossy leaves, divided into 5 toothed lobes* (often broader than illustrated). Its stems are 20-60 cm tall, topped in summer by a *branching inflorescence* of *pink or white flowers in ball-like clusters*, with a ruff of leafy bracts at the base of the branches. Its *egg-shaped fruits* are *covered in hooked bristles* for dispersal in fur or clothing. It grows in woods throughout the mainland and inner islands, but not on the W or N Isles.

Gael: *Bodan Coille* ('Little Penis/Tail of the Wood')

Pignut

Conopodium majus
CARROT FAMILY

Pignut's name comes from the *swollen, brown, edible tuber* at the base of its *wavy, shallowly-grooved stem*, which stands to about 40 cm tall. Its *leaves are triangular in outline and finely divided into narrow segments*, the basal ones withering as the flowers develop in early summer. The *white flowers* are arranged in a *neatly convex umbel* (see p. 30), which droops in bud, and usually lack bracts. The *oblong, brown fruits* are about 4 mm long. Pignut grows in open woodland and grassy places on acid soils throughout Scotland, although it is possibly introduced on the W Isles.

Gael: *Cnò-thalmhainn* ('Earth-nut')

Dog's Mercury

Mercurialis perennis
SPURGE FAMILY

This creeping perennial carpets the floors of well-established woods, almost exclusively S of the Great Glen, ascending to 1,000 m amongst shady mountain rocks. Its *unbranched, downy stems*, to 40 cm tall, have *opposite pairs of oval, toothed leaves*. The *flowers are 4 mm across, with 3 green lobes*, in spikes in the angles of the upper leaves in spring. Each patch of plants has either long spikes of male flowers (M above), with a tuft of yellowish stamens, or female flowers (F), without stamens, tucked amongst the upper leaves on short spikes which lengthen as the *hairy fruit capsules* develop.

Gael: Lus Glinne (possibly 'Plant of Cleansing')

Primrose

Primula vulgaris
PRIMROSE FAMILY

This familiar woodland flower (see p. 124) is found throughout Scotland, growing also in open, grassy places, including sea cliffs. It has basal rosettes of *crinkly, oblong, blunt-ended leaves*, to 25 cm long, which are *softly downy underneath and narrow gradually into a stalkless base*. Its flowers, on *long, shaggy stalks* in spring, have a *yellow petal-tube*, with *5 spreading, shallowly-notched lobes, about 3 cm in diameter*, surrounded by a *shaggy, cylindrical sepal-tube*. A *darker yellow 'eye'* encircles the contracted mouth of the petal-tube, in which are visible *either the stamens or stigmas*. (See also Cowslip, p. 76).

Gael: Sòbhrach (derivation obscure).

Yellow Pimpernel

Lysimachia nemorum
PRIMROSE FAMILY

This charming perennial *creeps* over the floors of shady woods and hedgerows throughout most of Scotland, although it is less common in C and NE Scotland, rare in Orkney and the W Isles, and absent from Shetland. It has slender, hairless stems to 40 cm long, with *opposite pairs of evergreen, pointed, oval leaves, rounded at the base.* It flowers in late spring and summer, producing solitary *pale yellow flowers with a deeper yellow 'eye' on fine stalks* arising from the angles of the leaves and just longer than them. Like primroses, the flowers are tubular at the base, with petal lobes *spreading out flat* to a diameter of about 12 mm.
Gael: *Seamrag Moire ('Mary's Shamrock')*

Creeping Jenny

Lysimachia nummularia
PRIMROSE FAMILY

Spreading into more open grassland than Yellow Pimpernel, this is another creeping plant, with rather tougher stems to 60 cm long. However, its *leaves are almost circular in outline, blunt-ended and dotted with black glands* and, in midsummer, it has *more cup-shaped, richer yellow, gland-dotted flowers,* which are 15-25 mm across and borne on *stout stalks shorter than the leaves.* It grows uncommonly in damp hedgebanks and grasslands, including gardens, only in the S and E.
Gael: *Lus Cùinneach ('Coin Plant')*

Lesser Periwinkle

Vinca minor
PERIWINKLE FAMILY

Mostly or exclusively a garden escape, originating from mainland Europe, this *evergreen, creeping shrub* has *trailing stems*, to 60 cm long, which *root at intervals* and give off short, erect flowering stems. It has *opposite pairs of short-stalked, glossy, oval, privet-like leaves* and produces solitary, *blue flowers* in spring. These are *25-30 mm across, with a long tube and 5 spreading, asymmetric lobes*. It grows in scattered woods and hedgerows, mostly in the S and E.

Gael: Faochag Bheag ('Small Periwinkle')

OTHER SPECIES: Greater Periwinkle (*V. major*), with *taller, more upright stems, rooting at their tips, longer-stalked leaves* and *flowers to 5 cm across* is a rare hedgerow introduction in the S and NE.

Green Alkanet

Pentaglottis sempervirens
BORAGE FAMILY

An introduction from SW Europe, this *roughly hairy perennial* grows in hedgerows and woodland margins locally in the S and E. It stands to 1 m tall with *broadly oval, pointed, net-veined leaves*. It resembles Comfrey (p. 171) in general appearance but with *bright blue flowers* borne in *bristly clusters* in early summer. The *tubular flowers* have 5 *sepal-teeth* and 5 *petal-lobes*, spreading to *about 1 cm in diameter*, with *white scales guarding the throat*. They resemble Bugloss flowers (p.55), but have a *straight, not kinked, petal-tube*.

Gael: Bog-lus ('Soft Plant')

141

Wood Forget-me-not

Myosotis sylvatica
BORAGE FAMILY

This *downy* biennial to perennial grows in damp woods in S and E Scotland and occasionally as a garden escape elsewhere. It stands to 45 cm tall with *oblong leaves covered with spreading hairs*, and typical forget-me-not inflorescences like scorpion tails (see p. 56) in early summer. It is distinguished from other forget-me-nots by its habitat, the *relative short flower stalks (about 1½ times as long as the sepal-tube)*, *the hooked hairs covering the sepal-tube* and the large *sky-blue flowers* which are 6-8 mm in diameter.

Gael: *Lus Midhe Coille ('Midhe – obscure – Plant of Woods')*

Common Cow-wheat

Melampyrum pratense
FIGWORT FAMILY

Cow-wheat is a partial parasite, with roots which tap those of other plants to draw nutrients. 8-60 cm tall, it has spreading branches and *opposite pairs of narrow, short-stalked leaves*. Its *tubular yellow flowers* develop in summer and early autumn *in pairs held horizontally and turned to face the same way*. The *11-15 mm long petal-tube* is twice as long as the sepal-tube, with the upper lip exceeding the lower and often tinged red. The plant grows in open woods, heaths and grassland throughout Scotland and the islands. (cf. Small Cow-wheat, p. 216).

Gael: *Càraid Bhuidhe ('Yellow Twins' or 'Yellow Couple')*

Common Figwort

Scrophularia nodosa
FIGWORT FAMILY

Figworts have *square stems*, opposite leaves and leafy clusters of flowers with a *globular, helmeted, rather dingy-coloured petal-tube*, which attracts pollinating wasps. This species has a *stout, hairless stem*, to 80 cm tall, which is *sharply angled but not winged*. Its *foul-smelling, pointed, oval leaves* have *coarsely-toothed margins* and *unwinged stalks*. Its petal-tubes are *greenish with a purplish-brown helmet* and its 5 sepal-lobes have a narrow pale border. It grows in damp woods and hedgerows throughout mainland Scotland and the inner islands.

Gael: *Lus nan Cnapan ('Knobbed Plant')*

OTHER SPECIES: Water Figwort (*S. auriculata*), with *winged stems and leaf stalks, bluntly-toothed leaves* and *broad pale margins to the sepal-lobes* grows in a few wet places in the E and far W. Green Figwort (*S. umbrosa*), with *even more strongly winged stems* and *sharply-toothed leaves* is rare in damp shady places in the S.

Yellow Figwort

Scrophularia vernalis
FIGWORT FAMILY

Introduced from C Europe to a few plantations in the SE, this is the only Scottish Figwort with *softly hairy, weakly-angled stems*. Its *deeply-toothed leaves* are *thin, wrinkled, and often yellowish-green*, and its *flowers, in springtime, are greenish-yellow without an obvious helmet* but with a *contracted throat*.

Gael: *Lus nan Cnapan an Earraich ('Spring Knobbed Plant')*

143

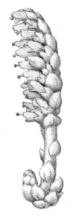

Toothwort

Lathraea squamaria
BROOMRAPE FAMILY

Completely lacking green, photosynthetic leaves, Toothwort obtains its food as a parasite on the roots of trees such as Elm, Hazel or Sycamore. As the sap rises in the host tree in spring, Toothwort produces clumps of *stout, unbranched, downy, flesh-coloured stems* to 30 cm tall, with a *few whitish scales* at their bases. These are topped by a *one-sided cluster* of stalked, pinkish, 2-lipped, tubular flowers with protruding stamens, in the angles of *fleshy, colourless bracts*. It grows in a few broadleaved woods in the S (cf. Bird's-nest Orchid, p. 153).
Gael: Slàn-fhiacail (possibly 'Tooth-healer')

OTHER SPECIES: The only true broomrape in Scotland is Thyme Broomrape (*Orobanche alba*), which is *usually purplish-red, with stalkless flowers* arranged *around the inflorescence*. It is a rare parasite on Thyme in rocky grassland in the far W and W islands.

Giant Bellflower

Campanula latifolia
BELLFLOWER FAMILY

The tallest Bellflower, reaching *1.2 m in height*, this softly hairy perennial grows in rich woodland and hedgerows, scattered through the lowlands. It has *bluntly-angled, unbranched stems*, and *toothed, egg-shaped leaves*, the lower with a *winged stalk* and the upper *stalkless*. The *purplish-blue bell-shaped flowers* in midsummer are *4 cm or more long*, with *petal-lobes almost as long as the tube at their base*.

Gael: Guc Mòr ('Large Bell')

Woodruff

Galium odoratum
BEDSTRAW FAMILY

Woodruff spreads by creeping runners to form *pale-green patches* in damp woodlands, in all but Highland areas and the Isles. It has unbranched, *4-angled stems* to 45 cm tall, with *whorls of 6-9 narrow leaves* with *forwardly-directed marginal prickles*. In early summer, the stems are topped by loose clusters of *fragrant, white, tubular flowers*, about 4 mm across, divided to about half-way into *4 narrow petal-lobes*. These develop into *round fruits, covered in hooked, black-tipped bristles*.
Gael: Lus a' Chaitheimh ('Plant of Consumption')

Honeysuckle

Lonicera periclymenum
HONEYSUCKLE FAMILY

Twining clockwise round tree trunks, Honeysuckle can reach heights of 6 m, although it also scrambles amongst shady rocks and hedgerows almost anywhere in Scotland, including the Isles. It has *downy, woody stems* and *opposite pairs of untoothed, oval leaves* which are *dark-green above and bluish beneath*. In summer, the stems are topped by *tight clusters of strongly 2-lipped flowers*, with *petal-tubes about 4 cm long, creamy-white inside and purplish or yellowish outside*. These develop in late summer into *glossy red berries*.
Gael: Lus na Meala ('Honey Plant') or Iadh-shlat ('Twig that Surrounds')

OTHER SPECIES: Fly Honeysuckle (*L. xylosteum*), a *bushy shrub* with *paired flowers*, and Perfoliate Honeysuckle (*L. caprifolium*), with *upper leaves fused round the stem*, are rare introductions in the SE.

Moschatel

Adoxa moschatellina
MOSCHATEL FAMILY

A delicate perennial of obscure relationships, Moschatel grows in rich woodland and amongst shady mountain rocks to high altitude, throughout the S and E. A far-creeping underground stem produces erect stems to 10 cm tall and *long-stalked root leaves* that are *neatly divided into 3 3-lobed leaflets*. The stem supports a *single, opposite pair of short-stalked, 3-lobed leaves*, and is topped in spring by *4 greenish flowers pointing at right angles and a 5th pointing vertically upwards*. The side flowers (illustrated) have 5 green petal-lobes and apparently 10 yellow stamens (in fact 5 divided in half) and the topmost flower has 4 petal-lobes and 8 apparent stamens.
Gael: *Mosgadal (as English, from French for its musky smell)*

Pyrenean Valerian

Valeriana pyrenaica
VALERIAN FAMILY

An introduction from the Pyrenees around the 17th century, this handsome alien was planted widely in the policy woods (see p. 126) of C and E Scotland as far N as Aberdeenshire, and is now well established in damp woodland and shady riversides. It is *taller than Common Valerian* (p 86), with *stout, hairy stems to 1.2 m tall*, broader, heart-shaped, undivided, coarsely-toothed lower leaves and *upper stem-leaves with 1 or 2 pairs of leaflets*. Its flowers, in midsummer, are similar to Common Valerian, but in slightly larger, denser heads.
Gael: *Carthan Curaidh Piorainidheach ('Pyrenean Warrior's Friendship')*

Leopardsbane

Doronicum pardalianches
DAISY FAMILY

This species, from W Europe, and 2 related garden hybrids were widely planted in policy woodlands (see p. 126) for their splashes of *yellow daisy flowers, about 5 cm across*, in spring and early summer. Dense patches still survive in woods today, widely in the E and less commonly in the W. They produce *basal rosettes of long-stalked, rounded, downy. toothed leaves with heart-shaped bases*. Their stems, to 90 cm tall, are *woolly with hairs* and bear several *rounded, toothed, pale green leaves*, the upper of which *clasp and half-enfold the stem at their base*.

Gael: Dìthean Buidhe Mòr ('Big Yellow Flower')

White Butterbur

Petasites albus
DAISY FAMILY

Originally introduced from C Europe for a flush of early spring colour in woodland, this patch-forming perennial has become a troublesome weed in woods in E Scotland, being especially noticeable beside the Glasgow to Edinburgh railway line. From *late February to May*, it produces *pyramidal spikes of dirty-white tubular flowers* without spreading ray-florets. These are followed by patches of *shallowly-lobed leaves, about 20 cm across*, which are *white-woolly with hairs underneath*. (cf Butterbur, p. 179).

Gael: Gallan Bàn ('White Branch')

OTHER SPECIES: Winter Heliotrope (*P. fragrans*), with *lilac flowerheads in late winter*, and *kidney-shaped, toothed but unlobed leaves*, forms patches on a few roadside banks and streamsides in the E.

147

Goldenrod

Solidago virgaurea
DAISY FAMILY

A native perennial of dry woodland and grassland, Goldenrod also grows on mountain rocks to high altitude throughout Scotland, including the Isles, although commoner in the W. It has leafy, little-branched stems to 75 cm tall, although much shorter in exposed mountain sites (variety *cambrica*), with *slightly-toothed, stalked, oblong lower leaves and narrower, unstalked upper leaves*. In mid- to late-summer, it produces *showy spikes* of *golden-yellow flowers*, up to 1 cm across, *with 6-12 spreading rays* and surrounded by *several rows of overlapping, greenish-yellow, papery-margined bracts*.
Gael: Slat Oir (as English)

Lily-of-the-Valley

Convallaria majalis
LILY FAMILY

Familiar in cultivation, this fragrant plant is native in a few, scattered lime-rich woodlands in C Scotland and the C Highlands, although its natural distribution is undoubtedly enhanced by introductions, especially in the SE. It spreads by far-creeping underground stems to form *dense patches* of *broadly oval root leaves*, which are 8-20 cm long and up to 5 cm across at their widest. Their twisted bases sheath a leafless flower-stem, to 25 cm tall, which appears in early summer and is topped by a *one-sided spike* of *6-12, nodding, bell-like white flowers*, 5-9 mm long. These develop into *round, red berries*.
Gael: Lili nan Gleann ('Lily of the Glens', from Biblical name)

Solomon's-seal

Polygonatum multiflorum
LILY FAMILY

This showy garden plant is a long-established introduction in a few woods in the S and E. It spreads by far-creeping underground stems, producing open patches of *hairless, arching stems*, to 80 cm long, with a *few, alternate, stalkless, oval stem leaves*. In the angles of the upper leaves in early summer it produces *hanging tassels of 1-6, nodding, tubular, greenish-white flowers*, 9-15 mm long, with constricted waists. These develop into *blue-black berries*.

Gael: *Seula Sholaimh Coitcheann* ('*Common Solomon's Seal*')

OTHER SPECIES: Whorled Solomon's-seal (*P. verticillatum*), with *whorls of 3-6 leaves around its upper stem* and greenish-white flowers *to 10 mm long* is a rare plant of mountain woods in the C Highlands.

Wild Hyacinth

Hyacinthoides non-scripta
LILY FAMILY

Known as Bluebell in England and Wild Hyacinth in Scotland, this familiar plant carpets a few woods in S Scotland, and occasionally forms blue sheets elsewhere after a wood is felled. More generally, it grows as scattered patches of *strap-shaped, glossy leaves*, to 45 cm long, in woods and shady gullies throughout Scotland except for Highland areas and the N Isles. In spring, its leafless flower-stalks are topped by a *one-sided spike of 4-16, nodding, violet-blue (rarely white or pink) bell-shaped flowers*, with petal-lobes bent back at the tip.

Gael: *Bròg na Cuthaig* ('*Cuckoo's Shoe*').

Ramsons

Allium ursinum
LILY FAMILY

Ramsons or Wild Garlic forms carpets of *bright green, tongue-shaped leaves*, 10-25 cm long and up to 8 cm broad, *smelling strongly of garlic when crushed*. In spring and early summer it produces *leafless, angled flower-stems*, to 45 cm tall, topped by a *flat-topped cluster of 6-20 long-stalked, starry white flowers*, with a 2-lobed papery bract beneath. It grows in damp woods and shady places, mostly in the S and W, being absent from most Highland areas and a rare garden escape in the N Isles.
Gael: Creamh (possibly from 'to gnaw/nibble')

Few-flowered Leek

Allium paradoxum
LILY FAMILY

This gregarious introduction (see p. 127) is abundant in a few woods in the SE and Moray coast, spreading by bulbils to form dense patches. The single leaf from each bulb is *narrower (5-25 mm wide), glossier and darker green* than that of Ramsons, and the inflorescence, on a *strongly 3-sided stem* in spring, has *1-4, long-stalked, starry white flowers*, intermixed with *numerous yellow bulbils*, protected by a *broad, brownish, papery bract*.
Gael: Creamh nan Lusan Gann ('Sparse-flowered Leek')

OTHER SPECIES: Wild Onion (*A. vineale*), with *hollow cylindrical leaves* and *greenish or reddish flowers intermixed with green or purple bulbils* or *with bulbils only*, grows in a few grassy places near S coasts.

Herb Paris

Paris quadrifolia
LILY FAMILY

This is the 'herb of parts', the numerical equality of its components supposedly showing its herbal powers to restore equanimity after epilepsy or witchcraft. From a creeping underground stem it produces hairless aerial stems to 40 cm tall with a *ring of usually 4, broad, unstalked, strongly-veined, oval leaves.* From the middle of these in early summer arises a single flower with *4 narrow green sepals, 4 shorter and narrower yellowish-green petals and 8 stamens,* developing into a *purplish-black berry.* It grows uncommonly in a few lime-rich woods, mostly in C Scotland and the C Highlands, with a single site in a limestone pavement on Skye.

Gael: Aon-dhearc ('One / Solitary Berry')

Snowdrop

Galanthus nivalis
LILY FAMILY

Native from France southwards but widely planted in woods and grassy banks throughout lowland Scotland, this delicate perennial has *narrow, bluish-green, strap-shaped leaves* about as long as the leafless flower-stalk. This is produced as the ice retreats in late winter and stands to 20 cm tall. It is topped by a solitary, nodding flower, which has *3 pure-white outer flower-lobes,* about 15 mm long, and *3, shorter inner flower-lobes,* which are *white with a green spot at their tip* and form an open bell-shape.

Gael: Gealag-làir ('Little White One of the Ground')

151

Great Woodrush

Luzula sylvatica
RUSH FAMILY

By far the largest Woodrush, this robust, densely-tufted plant forms *tussocks of bright green, strap-shaped leaves*, to 30 cm long by about 1 cm wide, *sparsely covered in white hairs*. From the tussocks in early summer arise flowering stems to 80 cm tall, topped by a *loosely-branched cluster* of *small, chestnut-brown flowers* in groups of 3 or 4. These have 2 whorls of 3 inconspicuous flower-lobes, about 3 mm long, and ripen to brown egg-shaped fruits. The plant grows in acid woodland, gullies, mountain rocks and clifftops throughout Scotland.

Gael: Luachair Coille ('Wood Rush')

Lords-and-Ladies

Arum maculatum
ARUM FAMILY

Also known as Cuckoo-pint or Wild Arum, this hairless perennial has *long-stalked, glossy. dark-green, arrow-shaped root-leaves*, which appear in early spring and are rarely black-spotted in Scotland. In later spring, a *pale, yellow-green or purple-edged sheath*, called the spathe, develops. This *completely encloses* the *purple-tipped flowering spike* or spadix, which has a ring of female flowers at its base and a ring of male flowers above, separated by a barrier of hairs which wither after pollination. Poisonous *berries* then develop, ripening from green to red. The plant forms patches in rich woodland from the Forth-Clyde valley southwards, and is an occasional introduction elsewhere up the E coast.

Gael: Cluas Chaoin ('Soft Ear')

Broad-leaved Helleborine

Epipactis helleborine
ORCHID FAMILY

This robust orchid grows in woods, clearings and long-established gardens in S Scotland and the far W. It has up to 3 stems, to 80 cm tall, which are *white-downy above and often purplish below* and have a spiral of *pointed, broadly oval leaves half-clasping the stem*. In late summer, it produces a *crowded, one-sided spike* of *15-50 flowers* with 3 narrow, green or dull-purple outer lobes, 2 pinkish upper lobes and a purple, heart-shaped lip with a bent-back tip.

Gael: Eileabor Leathann ('Broad Helleborine')

OTHER SPECIES: Dark-red Helleborine (*E. atrorubens*), with *2-ranked leaves* and *purple flowers* (p. 249), grows in limestone rocks in the NW. Narrow-lipped Helleborine (*E. leptochila*) and Young's Helleborine (*E. youngiana*), grow only on mining spoil heaps (bings) S of Glasgow.

Bird's-nest Orchid

Neottia nidus-avis
ORCHID FAMILY

Entirely lacking green leaves, this honey-coloured orchid relies on a fungus in its roots to absorb nourishment from the leaf-litter of shady woods in C Scotland and the C Highlands. Its stems, to 45 cm tall, are enwrapped by a few *papery, brown, sheathing leaves* and topped in early summer by a spike of *sickly-smelling brown flowers* with a *lower lip to 12 mm long, splitting into 2 blunt-ended lobes*. (cf Toothwort, p. 144).

Gael: Mogairlean Nead an Eòin (as English; Magairle see p. 206)

153

Marsh Marigold

Caltha palustris
BUTTERCUP FAMILY

Resembling a hefty buttercup, this hairless perennial forms splashes of yellow in spring in marshes, ditches, streamsides and wet woods throughout Scotland. Its flowers, which are *up to 5 cm across*, have *5-8 golden-yellow, petal-like lobes*, often greenish beneath, and *up to 100 stamens*, ripening to a cluster of *dry, brownish, pod-like fruits*. Its *glossy, kidney-shaped leaves* have a *wavy, toothed edge*. A smaller-flowered form with creeping stems grows beside mountain springs.

Gael: *Lus Buidhe Bealltainn ('Yellow Plant of Beltane (May Day)')*

Lesser Spearwort

Ranunculus flammula
BUTTERCUP FAMILY

Highly variable, this abundant plant of wet places throughout the mainland and islands has *small buttercup flowers*, to 2 cm across, on *grooved and slightly hairy stalks*, with 5 greenish-yellow sepals and 5 pale-yellow petals. Its *stems creep* amongst the vegetation, with shoots bending upwards, to 50 cm long, and *rather fleshy, lance-shaped leaves*, the upper of which are stalkless. The leaves, which are poisonous to cattle, have a burning taste (hence *flammula* meaning 'little flame').

Gael: *Glaisleun (possibly derived from 'green' and 'swamp')*

OTHER SPECIES: Greater Spearwort (*R. lingua*) *to 1.2 m tall with flowers to 5 cm across on grooveless but rather hairy stalks* grows in a few swamps in the S and E.

Ivy-leaved Water Crowfoot

Ranunculus hederaceus
BUTTERCUP FAMILY

Water Crowfoots are *water-living, white-flowered buttercups* with *rounded floating leaves* or *feathery underwater leaves* or both, but their form varies with habitat, making identification tricky. This is the commonest Scottish species, growing in wet mud and shallow water round most of the country. It has *smallish flowers, to 8 mm in diameter, fleshy, ivy-shaped floating leaves* and *no submerged leaves*.
Gael: Fleann Uisge Eidheannach ('Ivy-leaved Water Fleann' – see below)

Common Water Crowfoot

Ranunculus aquatilis
BUTTERCUP FAMILY

Frequent in ponds, ditches and slow-moving streams in the SE but uncommon elsewhere, this species has *floating leaves with 3-7 deeply-cut, wedge-shaped, toothed lobes, rounded feathery submerged leaves* and *flowers to 18 mm across*.
Gael: Fleann Uisge ('Water Fleann' – derivation obscure)

OTHER SPECIES: Round-leaved Water Crowfoot (*R. omiophyllus*), like Ivy-leaved but with *flowers to 15 mm across* and *roundish to kidney-shaped floating leaves*, grows in streams and mud in the SW. River Water Crowfoot (*R. fluitans*) with *only much-forked submerged leaves to 50 cm long,* and *flowers to 25 mm across* grows in fast-flowing S streams. Five other species occur rarely, including one in brackish coastal pools.

155

Celery-leaved Buttercup

Ranunculus sceleratus
BUTTERCUP FAMILY

The common name sums up this annual or overwintering herb, which has *shiny, toothed, deeply-lobed root leaves*, resembling celery, *narrower, less divided stem leaves*, and *small buttercup flowers* in summer, *less than 1 cm across*. These have *pale-yellow petals* and *bent-back sepals* and develop into an *oblong head of 70-100 tiny green fruits*. The *stout, hollow, grooved stems*, to 60 cm tall, grow in and around muddy ponds, streams and ditches, in the SE, Argyll and coastal areas N to the Moray Firth.
Gael: Torachas Biadhain (derivation obscure)

Watercress

Rorippa nasturtium-aquaticum
CABBAGE FAMILY

Also cultivated as green or summer cress, Watercress is native in streams, marshes and ponds around Scotland and the Isles. It has *creeping, rooting, dark-green to purple stems* and *hollow flower-stems*, which bend upwards to 60 cm tall or float on the water. Its leaves have *2-10 oval side leaflets, and a larger, rounder end leaflet*. Tight clusters of *white 4-petalled flowers*, around 6 mm across, appear in summer, ripening into *slightly curved pods, 11-19 mm long*. (cf. Fool's Watercress, p.167).
Gael: Biolair Uisge (as English; Biolair possibly from old word for 'water')

OTHER SPECIES: Narrow-fruited Watercress (*R. microphylla*), with *curved pods 16-23 mm long*, and a hybrid between these two, with distorted, *stubby, few-seeded pods*, are not uncommon in the E.

Marsh Yellow-cress

Rorippa palustris
CABBAGE FAMILY

This *hairless annual*, with *hollow, branching stems* to 60 cm tall, has *leaves divided into 5-13 wavy-edged lobes but not cut to the midrib*, often with *small ears clasping the stem* at the base of their stalks. Its flowers, in *loose heads* in summer and early autumn, are *3 mm across* with *4 pale-yellow petals*, ripening into an *oval pod, 5-10 mm long*. It grows in damp muddy places, almost entirely S of the Highland Boundary.

Gael: *Biolair Buidhe Lèana (as English)*

OTHER SPECIES: Creeping Yellow-cress (*R. sylvestris*), a *weak-stemmed, patch-forming perennial* with *crowded heads* of flowers *to 5 mm across* and *narrow, curved pods, 7-23 mm long*, grows in open, damp ground, scattered in SE, C and NE Scotland.

Cuckooflower

Cardamine pratensis
CABBAGE FAMILY

Also known as Lady's Smock, this graceful perennial, to 80 cm tall, can turn damp grassland, marshes, and ditches anywhere in Scotland into lilac sheets in spring and early summer, just as the cuckoo begins calling (hence its name). It resembles a large Wavy Bitter-cress (p.49), with similar *roundly-lobed leaves* in a basal rosette (and narrower-lobed stem leaves), but its flowers are *lilac, pale pink or white* and up to *2 cm across*, with *petals 2-3 times as long as the sepals*.

Gael: *Flùr na Cuthaig ('Flower of the Cuckoo')*

157

Blinks

Montia fontana
BLINKS FAMILY

This inconspicuous plant forms *low, compact tufts* on dry land and *straggling, rooting or floating stems*, to 50 cm long, in water. It has opposite pairs of *narrow, spatula-shaped leaves* on *reddish stems*. In summer and autumn, it produces *tiny white flowers, 3 mm across*, clustered at the stem tips, with 2 sepals and 5 *unequal petals*, ripening into *tiny, round fruit capsules*. It grows in springs, marshes, wet grassland and cut peat surfaces throughout Scotland.
Gael: Fliodh Uisge ('Water Chickweed')

Indian Balsam

Impatiens glandulifera
BALSAM FAMILY

Also known as Himalayan Balsam or Policeman's Helmet (from its flower shape), this robust annual with sturdy *reddish stems to 2 m tall* was introduced from the Himalayas in 1839, reaching Scotland by 1920. It is still spreading, forming patches on riverbanks and wasteground N to Shetland in the E and Fort William in the W. It has *toothed, lance-shaped leaves in whorls of 2-3, long-stalked, hooded, purplish-pink flowers*, shaped like Chinese lanterns, to 4 cm long, on long stalks from the angles of upper leaves in summer, and cylindrical fruits which *explode, scattering their waterborne seeds*.
Gael: Lus a' Chlogaid ('Helmet Plant')

OTHER SPECIES: Small Balsam (*I. parviflora*), an introduction from Asia, *under 1 m tall* with *unpaired, alternating leaves* and *pale-yellow flowers to 15 mm long*, is spreading near mainland coasts.

Meadowsweet

Filipendula ulmaria
ROSE FAMILY

The *frothy, branching, cream-coloured inflorescences* of this perennial appear abundantly in wet meadows, marshland and riverbanks throughout Scotland in summer. Its stems, to 1.2 m tall, support many *strong-smelling leaves*, divided into *5-11 stalked, toothed, oval leaflets*, with *small lobes between them*, and *often silver-hairy underneath*. The flowers, *5-10 mm across* with 5 sepals and 5 (or occasionally 6) *creamy-white petals*, grow in *densely-packed inflorescences* and develop into *spirally-twisted heads* of 6-10 dry fruits.

Gael: Cneas Chù Chulainn ('Waist belt of Cuchullin' – a Celtic hero of legend)

OTHER SPECIES: Dropwort (*F. vulgaris*), uncommon in base-rich grassland in the E, has *rosette leaves with 17-41, deeply-cut leaflets, a few smaller stem leaves* and *loosely-clustered flowers with 6 creamy-white petals*.

Marsh Cinquefoil

Potentilla palustris
ROSE FAMILY

The *creeping, woody underground stems* of this hairless perennial produce *open patches of upright stems*, to 45 cm tall. Its *long-stalked leaves*, often *bluish-green underneath*, have 3, 5 or 7, *oblong, toothed leaflets*, to 6 cm long, spreading like open fingers. In early summer, the stems are topped by an open inflorescence of flowers with 5 *deep-purple petals*, 5 *longer, purple sepals* and 5 *narrow, green bract-lobes*. The plant grows in marshes, bogs and wet moorland, scattered round Scotland.

Gael: Còig-bhileach Uisge ('Five-leaved One of Water')

Water Avens

Geum rivale
ROSE FAMILY

The rosette leaves of this *downy 10-60 cm tall perennial* show its affinity to Wood Avens (p. 135), with which it often hybridises. They have *3-6 pairs of oval, deeply-toothed side leaflets and a larger, rounded end leaflet.* The *few, smaller stem leaves* are *undivided or 3-lobed.* In summer, the *long-stalked, nodding, lantern-shaped flowers,* to 15 mm long, have *5 notched, peach-coloured petals* almost concealed by a *purple sepal-tube,* with a frill of united bracts. They ripen into *bur-like heads of hooked fruits.* The plant grows in marshes, riversides and damp ground throughout Scotland, although very rarely in the W Isles.
Gael: Machall Uisge (perhaps 'Large-headed Plant of Water')

Opposite-leaved Golden Saxifrage

Chrysosplenium oppositifolium
SAXIFRAGE FAMILY

This perennial of springs, stream-sides and wet ground throughout Scotland, except Shetland, forms *loose mats of creeping, rooting stems* with *opposite pairs of bluntly toothed, rounded, pale-green, sparsely-hairy leaves.* Its flowers, 3-4 mm across, have *no petals* but *4 or 5 greenish-yellow sepals* surrounded by a *cup-like frill of bright green bracts.*
Gael: Lus nan Laogh ('Plant of the Calves')

OTHER SPECIES: Alternate-leaved Golden Saxifrage (*C. alternifolium*), with *stouter, erect stems, long-stalked, more lobed leaves* and usually a *single stem leaf,* grows in marshy places in the S and E.

Grass-of-Parnassus

Parnassia palustris
SAXIFRAGE FAMILY

This handsome perennial, supposedly worthy of the Gods on Mount Parnassus, is not a grass but a relative of saxifrages. It produces an *erect tuft of long-stalked, pale-green, heart-shaped root-leaves*, from the centre of which in late summer emerge flower-stems to 30 cm tall, *clasped by a single, stalkless leaf*. The *flowers are white, veined* and 15-30 mm across, with *5 sepals, 5 petals and 5 stamens* interspersed with *5 frilly tufts* of sterile stamens. It grows in wet grassland, marshes and fens throughout Scotland, including the N Isles, but is rare in the NE and unconfirmed on the W Isles.

Gael: *Fionnan Geal ('Pleasant Little White One')*

Purple Loosestrife

Lythrum salicaria
LOOSESTRIFE FAMILY

Purple Loosestrife slightly resembles Rosebay Willowherb (p.21), but grows by water and has very different flowers. It stands to 1.2 m tall, with *narrow, pointed oval, downy leaves* in pairs or whorls of 3. In midsummer, its stems are topped by *dense, whorled spikes*, to 30 cm long, of flowers which are 10-15 mm across with a *greenish-purple, toothed sepal-tube, usually 6, narrow, purple petals*, and 12 stamens and 6 stigmas at different levels inside the flowers. These ripen into *oblong capsules*. The plant inhabits marshes, riverbanks and lochsides, mostly in the W, from Skye southwards, with scattered sites in the E.

Gael: *Lus na Sìochaint ('Plant of Peace')*

161

Willowherbs (*Epilobium* species, such as Hoary Willowherb, right) are perennials with narrow, toothed leaves and pinkish flowers with 4 petals, 8 stamens and a club-shaped or 4-lobed stigma. Their long, narrow fruit capsules split lengthwise to release many white-plumed seeds. They differ from Rosebay Willowherb (p.21) in having *at least their lowest leaves in opposite pairs* and *upright flowers* with *equally-sized petals*. Individual species are very variable and hybridise freely, but the leaf shape and form of hairs are usually diagnostic. (See also pp. 29 and 194).

Great Willowherb

Epilobium hirsutum
WILLOWHERB FAMILY

The tallest willowherb, this handsome plant has stems to *1.5 m tall, densely covered in spreading white hairs*. It has *opposite pairs of coarsely-toothed, hairy, lance-shaped leaves*, to 12 cm long, which *half-clasp and extend shortly down the stems*. These are topped in midsummer by a leafy inflorescence of *pinkish-purple flowers, 15-25 mm across*, with *shallowly-notched petals* and a *cream-coloured stigma with 4 downcurved lobes*. It grows on streamsides and in marshes in the S and E.
Gael: Seileachan Mòr (as English)

OTHER SPECIES: Hoary Willowherb (*E. parviflorum*) (see box above) is shorter, to *60 cm tall*, with *mostly unpaired, non-clasping leaves* and *pale-pink flowers, to 10 mm across*, with *deeply-notched petals* and *flat stigma lobes*. It grows in similar habitats, scattered throughout Scotland.

Short-fruited Willowherb

Epilobium obscurum
WILLOWHERB FAMILY

This locally common willowherb grows in marshes, streamsides and wet woods throughout Scotland, including the W Isles, Orkney, and as a recent colonist on Shetland. Its stems are 30-60 cm tall, *downy above* and *marked with 4 raised lines* running down from the *stalkless base* of the *spear-shaped leaves*. Its *purplish-pink midsummer flowers* are 6-8 mm across with *shallowly-notched petals*, a *club-shaped stigma*, and a *sticky-haired sepal-tube*. The *downy fruit capsule* is 4-6 cm long.
Gael: *Seileachan Fàireagach* ('*Glandular Willowherb*')

OTHER SPECIES: Pale Willowherb (*E. roseum*), with *curly-haired stems* *with 2 distinct raised lines, stalked leaves*, and *flowers to 6 mm across* with *2-lobed petals, at first white then streaked pink*, and a *club-shaped stigma*, grows in damp places and wasteground in C and NE Scotland.

Marsh Willowherb

Epilobium palustre
WILLOWHERB FAMILY

Marsh Willowherb spreads by thin runners in marshes and bogs all round Scotland. It has *downy stems* to 60 cm tall, sometimes with *2 lines of curly hairs*, and *unstalked, lance-shaped leaves*, to 7 cm long, mostly in *opposite pairs*. Its midsummer *flowers*, *held almost horizontally*, are 4-6 mm across with *pale rose or white*, *shallowly-notched petals* and a *club-shaped stigma*, ripening to a *downy capsule*, 5-8 cm long.

Gael: *Seileachan Lèana* (*as English*)

163

Water Purslane

Lythrum portula
LOOSESTRIFE FAMILY

Improbably related to Purple Loosestrife (p.161), this *low, hairless annual* has *4-angled, reddish, rooting stems*, 4-25 cm long, which *creep* through muddy pool edges, puddles and wet, open ground, scattered over most of Scotland except the NW and Shetland. It has opposite pairs of *fleshy, spoon-shaped leaves, never in rosettes*, and *minute green flowers*, tucked in the angles of most leaves in summer and autumn. These have *6 petals which soon drop*, a *6-toothed sepal-tube* and *6 or 12 stamens*.
Gael: *Flùr Bogaich Ealaidheach* ('Creeping Bog Plant')

Alternate Water-milfoil

Myriophyllum alterniflorum
WATER-MILFOIL FAMILY

In summer, the spikes of Water-milfoil project from lochs, streams and ditches, mostly in the NW and Isles. Its slender, branching shoots, to 1.2 m tall, have *whorls of 4 (sometimes 3) leaves, divided into 6-18 feathery segments*. The tiny flowers, in groups of 1-4 in the angles of leafy bracts, form spikes to *3 cm long*. The *male upper flowers*, 4 mm across, have *8 stamens* and *4 red-streaked, yellowish petals*, which soon fall, while the *lower flowers are petalless females*.
Gael: *Snàthainn Bhàthaidh* ('Thread of Drowning')

OTHER SPECIES: Spiked Water-milfoil (*M. spicatum*) with *whorls of 4 leaves with 13-38 segments* and *flower-spikes longer than 4 cm*, grows in similar habitats mostly in the S and E.

Marestail

Hippuris vulgaris
MARESTAIL FAMILY

Unlike the similar Horsetails – a group of fern allies which reproduce by spores from terminal cones – Marestail has *tiny, green, petalless flowers* with red anthers, in the angles of its aerial leaves. Its stems, to 75 cm or more in height, are mostly submerged, with only a portion above the surface, and have *tight whorls of 6-12 soft, strap-like, unbranched leaves*. It grows in a few lochs, ponds and slow-moving streams, mostly in the S and E, but also the W and N Isles.
Gael: *Earball Capaill (as English)*

Common Water Starwort

Callitriche stagnalis
WATER STARWORT FAMILY

Several confusingly similar species of Water Starwort grow in Scotland. Some are entirely aquatic, while others, like this one, can have long, weak stems supported by the water of ponds, ditches and slow-moving streams, or shorter stems creeping through wet mud. They have *opposite pairs of narrow underwater leaves*, while their *floating or terrestrial leaves*, if present, are *oval and often form rosettes*. Their *tiny flowers*, in the angles of submerged or floating leaves, have no petals or sepals, but 1 stamen and 2 styles, sometimes with 2 crescent-shaped bracts beneath. This is the commonest species in ponds, ditches and wet mud throughout Scotland.
Gael: *Biolair Ioc (possibly 'Cress of Healing')*

165

Marsh Pennywort

Hydrocotyle vulgaris
CARROT FAMILY

An atypical umbellifer, Marsh Penny-wort spreads by *slender, creeping, rooting stems* which produce *wavy-edged, circular leaves*, 8-35 mm across, on *stalks to 25 cm tall attached centrally on the leaf's underside*. The *tiny flowers*, 1 mm across, in clusters in early summer, have 5 *green or pinkish petals*. They develop into *brown-dotted, pumpkin-shaped fruits*, about 2 mm across. Pennywort grows in bogs and marshes throughout Scotland.

Gael: *Lus na Peighinn* ('Penny Plant')

Hemlock Water-dropwort

Oenanthe crocata
CARROT FAMILY

This stout, hairless, *parsley-smelling* perennial resembles Hemlock (opposite) – and is equally poisonous – but it *grows in or by water* and has hollow, ridged, *green stems*. It stands to 1.5 m tall, with *leaves 3 times divided* into *wedge-shaped lobes* and *slightly sheathing the stem*. Its typical umbels (see p. 30) in early summer are 5-10 cm across with *12-40 rays* and *about 5 bracts*. The outer petals extend into a frill, and the *cylindrical fruits are about 3 mm long with 2 'horns'*.

Gael: *Dàtha Bàn Iteodha* ('White Hemlock'; *Dàtha* – obscure)

OTHER SPECIES: Parsley Water-dropwort (*O. lachenalii*), with *parsley-like leaves*, 5-9 *rays* and *shorter, egg-shaped fruits*, grows in brackish and freshwater marshes in the far W.

Hemlock

Conium maculatum
CARROT FAMILY

Poisonous in all its parts, Hemlock is identifiable by its grooved, *purple-spotted stems*, the *mousy smell of its foliage* when crushed, and its *round fruits*, about 3 mm long, with *wavy ridges*. It stands to 3 m tall, with *finely-cut, fern-like leaves* and *spreading inflorescences*, to 5 cm across, with *10-20 rays* and a *few, downturned bracts*. It grows in damp places, hedgebanks and rubbish tips in the E, W coasts and W islands, but is rare in the N and the Isles.

Gael: Iteodha (*perhaps from ite = 'feather'*)

Lesser Marshwort

Apium inundatum
CARROT FAMILY

This easily-overlooked, *straggling or floating perennial* grows partly or completely submerged in lochs, ponds and ditches, rarely far from E or W coasts. Its *weak, hairless stems* can be up to 75 cm long, with *submerged leaves finely divided into thread-like segments* and *aerial leaves usually with about 7 3-lobed leaflets*. The *inflorescences branch off the stem opposite a leaf* in summer, and have *2-4 rays* and *no bracts*. The white flowers develop into *oblong, ridged fruits* to 3 mm long.

Gael: Fualastar (*possibly 'Moist One', from fual = urine*)

OTHER SPECIES: Fool's Watercress (*A. nodiflorum*), with *leaves similar to those of Watercress* (p. 156) but *finely toothed*, *white-flowered inflorescences with 3-15 rays* and *ridged, egg-shaped fruits*, is uncommon in ditches and ponds in the S and W.

167

Cowbane

Cicuta virosa
CARROT FAMILY

This poisonous perennial grows uncommonly in shallow water and marshes beside lochs in the Borders, C Scotland and at one site on S Uist. It can be up to 1.5 m tall, with *ridged, hairless, hollow stems*. Its *leaves* are much-divided into *sharply-toothed, spear-shaped segments*, with *long stalks slightly sheathing the stem*. Its *inflorescences, branching from opposite leaves* in late summer, are 7-13 cm across, with *10-30 rays, no bracts* but *narrow bracteoles*. The *globular, slightly ridged fruits* are 2 mm long, retaining a *collar of sepal-teeth* and *2 long styles*.
Gael: Fealladh Bog ('Soft Deception')

Giant Hogweed

Heracleum mantegazzianum
CARROT FAMILY

Introduced to Victorian gardens, this massive alien escaped and spread along railways and rivers. Today it grows, often abundantly, by rivers and in wasteground as far N as Inverness on the E coast and in the SW (see p. 128). Its *hollow, hairy, purple-spotted stems* reach 5 m tall and 10 cm across, with *leaves to 2.5 m long, divided into broad, deeply-toothed lobes*. The umbrella-shaped inflorescences in early summer can be *50 cm across*, with *50-150 hairy rays* and *white or pinkish flowers*, ripening into *oval, winged fruits* about 1 cm long.
Gael: Odharan Mòr ('Large Dun-coloured One')
Giant Hogweed should not be handled, since contact with its sap sensitises the skin to sunlight, causing severe sunburn.

Amphibious Bistort

Persicaria amphibia
KNOTWEED FAMILY

Different forms of this perennial grow on land and in water, but both have *slender spikes*, 2-4 cm long, of *small pale-pink flowers* in summer. The *aquatic form* has *floating stems* to 50 cm long, with *dangling roots along their length*, and *floating oblong leaves*, 5-15 cm long, *abruptly cut off at the base*. The *terrestrial form* (illustrated) has upright stems, rooting only low down, and *downy leaves narrowed to a rounded base*. The plant grows in or beside ponds, canals and slow-flowing rivers around Scotland, although rarely in the C and NW Highlands.
Gael: Glùineach an Uisge ('Jointed One of the Water')

Water Pepper

Persicaria hydropiper
KNOTWEED FAMILY

Most easily told by the *biting taste* of its leaves, Water Pepper is an annual with *weak stems*, 25-75 cm long. At the base of its *almost stalkless, narrow lance-shaped, rough-edged leaves*, which are 3-9 cm long, the stem is enwrapped by a *papery, brown sheath* and often *swollen*. The *slender, leafy, nodding inflorescences* in late summer have many *flowers with usually 5 greenish lobes*, around 3 mm long, *covered in yellowish glands*. The plant grows round ponds and lochs and in damp places around most of Scotland except the N and N Isles.
Gael: Glùineach Theth ('Hot Jointed One')
The acrid sap of Water Pepper can irritate the skin.

Monk's Rhubarb

Rumex pseudoalpinus
DOCK FAMILY

Introduced from C Europe for veterinary use, this rhubarb-like perennial is widespread along streams and roadsides in E Highland glens, usually near farms or buildings. It forms patches of *long-stalked, wavy-edged. heart-shaped leaves* (without the fleshy red stalks of rhubarb). In summer, it has *greenish-yellow, spindle-shaped docken-like inflorescences*, to 1 m tall and *leafy near their bases*. The *fruit valves* (see p.34) are *egg-shaped, without warts*.
Gael: *Lus na Purgaid* ('Purgative Plant')

Yellow Loosestrife

Lysimachia vulgaris
PRIMROSE FAMILY

This *robust perennial*, to 1.5 m tall, forms patches on loch shores, riverbanks and marshland around Scotland except for the W and N Isles. Its *downy leaves, in whorls of 2-4*, are *lance-shaped, almost stalkless, 3-10 cm long*, and often *black- or orange-dotted*. Its *flowers, in a narrow, branching inflorescence* in midsummer, are about 15 mm across, with a *5-lobed petal-tube* and 5 *orange-rimmed sepal-teeth*.
Gael: *Seileachan Buidhe* ('Yellow Willowherb', *from leaf shape*)

OTHER SPECIES: Tufted Loosestrife (*L. thyrsiflora*), with *feathery spikes*, in leaf angles, of *7-lobed, black-dotted, yellow flowers, 5 mm across*, is a rare native of marshland in C Scotland. Fringed Loosestrife (*L. ciliata*), with *stalked, bristle-edged leaves* and *yellow flowers 25 mm across*, is sometimes naturalised near buildings, and Dotted Loosestrife (*L. punctata*), with *leaves and yellow petals fringed with hairs*, is a rare riverbank alien.

Brookweed

Samolus valerandi
PRIMROSE FAMILY

Confined to streams, ditches and marshes near W coasts, from the Solway to the W Isles, and E coasts mostly S of the Forth, this *hairless, pale-green perennial* rarely exceeds 25 cm tall. Its *spoon-shaped leaves*, to 8 cm long, grow in a *basal rosette* and *spiral alternately* up the stem. In summer, it has a *branching spike* of *long-stalked, white flowers*, about 3 mm across, with *5 petals joined half-way into a cup-shaped tube.*

Gael: *Luibh an t-Sruthain* ('Plant/Weed of the Stream')

Common Comfrey

Symphytum officinale
BORAGE FAMILY

Clumps of this *roughly-hairy perennial*, to 1.2 m tall, grow in damp places by rivers and streams in lowland Scotland, often as escapes from cultivation (for herbal use to stop bleeding and knit bones). Its *oval leaves*, to 25 cm long, are *stalkless, with their bases running down the stem as wide wings.* Its *purplish or creamy flowers*, in a *nodding, spirally-curved inflorescence* in early summer, have a *funnel-shaped, 5-lobed petal-tube*, 12-18 mm long, and *sepal-teeth twice as long as their tube.*

Gael: *Meacan Dubh* ('Black Plant')

OTHER SPECIES: Tuberous Comfrey (*S. tuberosum*), with *unwinged stems, yellow flowers* and *even longer sepal-teeth*, grows in similar places. Russian Comfrey (*S. x uplandicum*), introduced for fodder, with *bristly leaves, short stem-wings never reaching the next leaf*, and *blue to violet or pinkish flowers*, is commoner on lowland roadsides.

171

Water Forget-me-not

Myosotis scorpioides
BORAGE FAMILY

The commonest aquatic forget-me-not, this grows by streams and ponds over most of Scotland. Its creeping runners produce stems to 45 cm tall with *some spreading hairs and some appressed against the stem*. It has *downy, oval leaves*, to 10 cm long, and typical forget-me-not inflorescences (p.56) in summer, with a sky-blue petal-tube *4-8 mm across, and a sepal-tube longer than the style, with broad triangular teeth*.

Gael: Cotharach (perhaps 'Protector')

OTHER SPECIES: Creeping Forget-me-not (M. *secunda*) with *spreading hairs low on the stem, narrow sepal-teeth* and a *short style*, grows in wet peaty places. Tufted Forget-me-not (M. *laxa*), with *appressed stem hairs* and *flowers under 5 mm across*, grows in marshes and pond margins.

Monkey-flower

Mimulus guttatus
FIGWORT FAMILY

The commonest of several *Mimulus* garden escapes (see also p. 129), this grows commonly in streambanks throughout Scotland, especially in the E. It has *sprawling or ascending stems*, with *broad, irregularly-toothed leaves*, the upper of which are stalkless. Its *showy yellow flowers* in summer have a *long petal-tube and 2 prominent lips*. The upper lip is 2-lobed and the lower 3-lobed, *with red dots near the almost-closed throat*.

Gael: Meilleag an Uillt ('Blubber-lip of the Stream')

Brooklime

Veronica beccabunga
FIGWORT FAMILY

Jokingly said to earn its scientific name because it 'bungs up becks' (streams), this *hairless perennial* often forms dense patches in slow-moving streams, ditches, ponds and marshes in the S and E and the N Isles, but more rarely in the NW and W Isles. Its *stems*, to 60 cm long, *creep and root at the base*, then ascend, with *opposite pairs* of rather *fleshy, toothed, short-stalked, oval leaves*. In summer, *opposite pairs of inflorescences* emerge from the angles of the upper leaves, with *10-30* blue speedwell flowers (see p.80), *5-7 mm across*.

Gael: *Lochal Mothair (may be 'Loch Plant' – Mothair obscure)*

Marsh Speedwell

Veronica scutellata
FIGWORT FAMILY

This straggling plant inhabits ponds, bogs and wet grassland scattered throughout Scotland. Rarely more than 15 cm tall, it has *narrow, stalkless leaves*, to 4 cm long, *slightly clasping the stem* and often purple-tinged. In the angles of upper paired leaves in summer it produces *single, branching inflorescences* with *up to 10, long-stalked, white, pale blue or pinkish flowers*, 5-6 mm across.

Gael: *Lus-crè Lèana ('Marsh Dust-weed')*

OTHER SPECIES: Water Speedwell (*V. anagallis-aquatica*), with *broader, short-stalked leaves* and *paired inflorescences of 10-50 pale-blue flowers*, grows in similar habitats near coasts. Pink Water Speedwell (*V. catenata*) with *narrow, stalkless leaves* and *paired inflorescences of pink flowers* is uncommon near coasts and on W islands.

173

MINTS

Mints (*Mentha* species), such as Corn Mint (right), have a petal-tube with 4 nearly-equal lobes (unlike the typical 2-lipped flowers of the Thyme Family) and a sepal-tube with 4-5 equal teeth. The small, bell-shaped flowers grow in dense inflorescences. The aromatic plants spread by runners, forming patches in wet places. They hybridise freely, and the hybrids (often cultivated for culinary use) can persist by runners without either parent present.

Water Mint

Mentha aquatica
THYME FAMILY

The commonest Scottish mint, this *usually hairy* perennial grows in ponds, ditches, streams, marshes and wet woodland around Scotland, except for parts of the C and NW Highlands. It has *purple stems*, 15-90 cm tall, with pairs of *mint-scented, stalked, toothed, oval leaves*, 2-6 cm long. The *lilac-pink flowers*, with *long, obvious stamens* and a *downy sepal-tube* with 5 triangular teeth, grow in summer and early autumn in a *rounded head* (denser than illustrated) topping the stem, usually with *2 or 3 flower clusters in the angles of lower leaf pairs*.
Gael: *Meannt an Uisge* (as English)

OTHER SPECIES: Corn Mint (*M. arvensis*), illustrated in box above, has *sickly-smelling, narrow, hairy leaves*, a *leafy stem-tip*, *lilac flowers* clustered in the *angles of lower leaves, hairy sepal-tubes* with *narrow teeth to 2 mm long*, and *long stamens*. It grows less commonly in damp arable fields scattered around Scotland except for Highland areas and the N. Isles.

Spear Mint

Mentha spicata
THYME FAMILY

Scattered in damp disturbed ground through S and E Scotland, this *spearmint-smelling plant* is a garden escape. Its *hairless stems*, to 90 cm tall, have *opposite pairs* of *slightly hairy, lance-shaped, almost unstalked leaves*, with *forward-directed teeth*. Its *pink or white flowers*, with *narrow, hairy sepal-teeth to 3 mm long* and *long stamens*, appear in late summer in *spikes topping the stems*, with *needle-like bracts* beneath the *interrupted flower clusters*.

Gael: Meannt Gàrraidh (as English)

OTHER SPECIES: Whorled Mint, the Water x Corn Mint hybrid, resembles Corn Mint but has *small clusters, almost to the stem tip, of flowers with narrow, hairy sepal-teeth to 4 mm long and short stamens*; it is widespread by ditches and ponds. Peppermint, the Water x Spear Mint hybrid, with a *peppermint smell, hairless purple stems and spikes of flowers with hairless sepal-tubes with pointed teeth and short stamens*, is widespread in ditches and roadsides.

Gipsywort

Lycopus europaeus
THYME FAMILY

This *slightly hairy*, mint-like perennial, to 1 m tall, has *unstalked, lance-shaped leaves*, to 10 cm long, with *narrow, forward-directed lobes*. Its *flowers, clustered at the leaf bases*, have a *5-toothed sepal-tube* almost enclosing a *white petal-tube with 4, similar-sized, purple-dotted lobes*. It grows in marshes and watersides in the W and near E coasts.

Gael: Feòran Curraidh (perhaps 'Green Marsh Plant')

175

Marsh Woundwort

Stachys palustris
THYME FAMILY

Resembling Hedge Woundwort (p.38), but *not foul-smelling* when crushed, Marsh Woundwort has *paler pinkish-purple flowers* and *narrower, lance-shaped, almost completely stalkless, hairy leaves*, 5-12 cm long. In summer, its *hollow stems*, 40-100 cm tall, are topped by many *whorls of 6 flowers*, with leafy bracts beneath, clustered into a *dense spike* with a *few, more distant whorls* below. Its flowers are *2-lipped with a blotched lower lip*. It grows in marshes, ditches and streamsides throughout Scotland, but more rarely in the NW.

Gael: *Brisgean nam Caorach* ('Brittle One of the Sheep')

Skullcap

Scutellaria galericulata
THYME FAMILY

A plant of streamsides, fens and water-meadows, Skullcap is common in the W and W islands, scattered elsewhere and absent from Shetland. A *downy* perennial, with stems to 50 cm high from a creeping underground stem, it has *short-stalked, bluntly-toothed, spear-shaped leaves*, 2-5 cm long. In summer *pairs of flowers hang to one side* from leaf-like bracts in the upper stem. They have a *2-lipped, blue-violet petal-tube*, 10-20 mm long, *much longer than the 2-lipped sepal-tube*.

Gael: *Cochall* ('Husk' or 'Hood')

OTHER SPECIES: Lesser Skullcap (*S. minor*), with *untoothed leaves to 3 cm long* and a *pinkish-purple petal-tube less than 1 cm long*, is confined to wet heaths in the far W and islands.

176

Marsh Bedstraw

Galium palustre
BEDSTRAW FAMILY

This *straggling, hairless* perennial with slender, *rough-angled stems*, 15-100 cm tall, has whorls of 4-6 *blunt-ended, lance-shaped, prickly-margined leaves*, to 1 cm or longer, which *blacken when dried*. In midsummer, it produces *spreading, branched clusters* of white bedstraw flowers (p.40), 2.5-5 mm across. It grows in marshes, fens and wet meadows commonly throughout Scotland. Larger plants more than 30 cm tall with leaves over 2 cm long, are placed in subspecies *elongatum*.

Gael: Màdar Lèana ('Marsh Madder')

OTHER SPECIES: Fen Bedstraw (*G. uliginosum*) of fens (rich peatlands) in the Borders and S Highlands has *whorls of 6-8 leaves ending in a long point*, with *backward-pointing marginal prickles*, and white flowers *2.5 mm across*.

Marsh Valerian

Valeriana dioica
VALERIAN FAMILY

Smaller than Common Valerian (p.86), this slender marsh plant is confined to the far S. Its *creeping runners* produce *long-stalked, untoothed, oval root leaves* and stems to 30 cm tall. These are *slightly hairy* around where the *unstalked, deeply-lobed stem leaves* are attached. In early summer, the stems are topped by a *branching inflorescence* of *funnel-shaped pink flowers*. The male flowers, *about 5 mm across with obvious stamens*, grow on separate plants from the *female flowers*, 2 mm across with a 3-branched style, which ripen to a *round nutlet*.

Gael: Caoirin Lèana ('Little Berry of the Marsh')

177

Wild Teasel

Dipsacus fullonum
TEASEL FAMILY

Widely used in dried flower arrangements and native in England, Teasel has become established in wasteground, rubbish tips and riverbanks around the lowlands and is sometimes planted to provide wild bird seed. A robust, *prickly biennial*, to 1.5 m tall, it has *undivided, oblong basal leaves* which die before flowering, and pairs of *narrower, wavy-edged stem-leaves* overlapping at their base into a *water-holding cup*. In summer it produces *egg-shaped inflorescences*, to 8 cm long, *overtopped by long, curved prickly bracts* and densely covered in *shorter prickle-tipped flower bracts*, with *purplish petal-tubes* half-hidden amongst them.
Gael: *Leadan an Fhùcadair* ('Fuller's Locks', cf Burdock, p.41)

OTHER SPECIES: Fuller's Teasel (*D. sativus*) with *shorter, spreading inflorescence bracts* and *hook-tipped flower bracts* is occasional on tips.

Marsh Ragwort

Senecio aquaticus
DAISY FAMILY

The only ragwort of marshes and wet grassland in Scotland, Marsh Ragwort is widespread except in the C Highlands. It is shorter (to 80 cm) and less stiff than Common Ragwort (p.59), and has *less divided leaves, often purplish underneath*, with a *large end-lobe* and a *few forward-pointing side lobes*. At least some *basal leaves are almost undivided*, the lower stem leaves are stalked and the *upper stalkless*. The inflorescence in midsummer is *more open and wide-branching*, with larger golden-yellow daisy flowers, *25-40 mm across*.
Gael: *Caoibhreachan* ('Impediment', from cuibhreach = chain)

178

Butterbur

Petasites hybridus
DAISY FAMILY

The only native butterbur (cf p. 147), this forms dense patches of *long-stalked, toothed, heart-shaped, rhubarb-like leaves*, to 90 cm across and *greyish underneath*. Before the leaves develop in spring, it produces *cone-shaped inflorescences* on *sturdy stems* to 40 cm tall, covered in *green strap-shaped bracts*, with many *tufted, rayless, pale reddish-violet flowerheads*. 'Male' plants, which are much commoner (with a few female flowers), have *about 50 flowerheads, 7-12 mm long. Female plants, with up to 100 heads, 3-6 mm long*, are much rarer. Butterbur largely spreads by root fragments in disturbed ground by rivers and streams around the lowlands, W Isles and Orkney, but not in the C Highlands or Shetland.

Gael: Gallan Mòr ('Large Branch')

Marsh Cudweed

Gnaphalium uliginosum
DAISY FAMILY

A *low, bushy annual*, Marsh Cudweed has *sprawling, much-branched stems* to 20 cm long, with *narrow, grey, cottony leaves* and topped in summer by a *dense cluster of 3-10 rayless daisy heads*, 3-4 mm long, shorter than the surrounding leaves. The heads have a *central tuft of yellow florets*, surrounded by a *cone-shaped cup of brown bracts*. The plant grows in sporadically wet, open ground around Scotland and the Isles, except for the C Highlands. (cf Heath Cudweed, p.205; Dwarf Cudweed, p. 227)

Gael: Cnàmh-lus Lèana (as English)

179

Tansy

Tanacetum vulgare
DAISY FAMILY

Formerly cultivated for use against stomach pains and worms, Tansy is an *aromatic perennial* with *stiff, purplish stems* to 1.2 m tall and *leaves* to 25 cm long, *finely divided into toothed lobes*, with the *uppermost leaves stalkless*. In summer, it produces *dense, flat-topped inflorescences* of *button-like, rayless, golden-yellow flowerheads, 7-12 mm across*. It grows on roadsides, hedgerows and wasteground, scattered around Scotland, and as a garden escape on the Isles.
Gael: Lus na Frainge ('Plant of France')

OTHER SPECIES: Feverfew (*T. parthenium*), with *less-divided leaves* and *white-rayed daisy flowers*, grows on waysides and wasteground mainly in the E.

Water-plantain

Alisma plantago-aquatica
WATER-PLANTAIN FAMILY

This aquatic perennial has a *basal tuft* of *long-stalked, broadly oval, plantain-like leaves* and *leafless flowering stems*, 20-100 cm tall, topped in summer by *several whorls* of *long, branching flowerstalks*. The *flowers are 7-12 mm across*, with *3 pale-lilac petals* and *3 sepals*. It grows on mud in shallow water, mostly in C and S Scotland, more rarely in the N.
Gael: Corr-chopag (Copag = 'Little Tufted One' (cf Docks, p. 34); Corr obscure)

OTHER SPECIES: Lesser Water-plantain (*Baldellia ranunculoides*), with *narrow leaves* and *2 whorls of pale-pink flowers 10-16 mm across*, is rarer in similar habitats in C and NE Scotland and W islands.

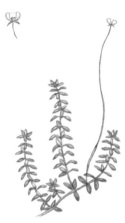

Canadian Pondweed

Elodea canadensis
FROGBIT FAMILY

Discarded from fish tanks, this *submerged aquatic*, first found in the wild in 1836, is common in slow-moving freshwater in the lowlands (and rare on Orkney). It has *brittle stems* to 3 m long, with *whorls of 3 oblong, finely-toothed, translucent leaves*, 5-12 mm long. It infrequently produces *floating female flowers* (illustrated), about 5 mm across with *3 narrow white or pale-purple petals. Male flowers*, produced on separate plants and *breaking off to float freely*, are even rarer.
Gael: *Linne-lus Canèideanach (from English)*

Bog Pondweed

Potamogeton polygonifolius
PONDWEED FAMILY

At least 17 species of Pondweeds grow in Scotland, 5 of which are widespread, but this is the commonest, growing in bog-pools, ditches and ponds almost throughout the country. All produce rather knobbly *spikes*, held above the water in summer, of *tiny greenish flowers* with 4 sepals, *no petals* and 4 stamens. The spikes often sink as the fruits, of *4 nutlets*, develop. Some species have floating leaves and differently-shaped submerged leaves, others only submerged leaves, but the leaf shape can vary with depth and speed of the water and even the plant's age, and the species hybridise freely, making identification complex. This species has *reddish, oval floating leaves and spear-shaped submerged leaves.*
Gael: *Lìobhag Bogaich ('Small Polished One of the Bog')*

181

Yellow Iris

Iris pseudacorus
IRIS FAMILY

Yellow (Flag) Iris forms dense patches of *ridged, sword-shaped, rather bluish-green leaves*, 40 cm or more long and up to 3 cm across. In early summer, *stout flowering stems* to 1 m tall develop, topped by a branching inflorescence of *4-12 showy, yellow flowers* to 10 cm across, with leaf-like bracts. The flowers are complex in structure, with 3 *broad, down-turned outer flower-lobes*, marked with *red veins*, 3 *upright, twisted inner lobes*, with 3 *petal-like style branches*. The plant is common in wet ground throughout Scotland.
Gael: Seileasdair or Sealasdair (derivation obscure)

Common Duckweed

Lemna minor
DUCKWEED FAMILY

This tiny, floating waterplant sometimes forms green sheets over ponds, ditches and canals, mostly S of the Highland boundary and is more scattered in the NE, NW, and W and N Isles. A *single root*, to 15 cm long, dangles below each *rounded, 3-veined frond*, 1.5-5 mm across. On top of its fronds it irregularly produces *minute greenish flowers*, with 2 male flowers and 1 female *enclosed by a sheath*. It reproduces mainly by budding off new fronds and is spread on birds' feet.
Gael: Mac gun Athair ('Fatherless Son')

OTHER SPECIES: Ivy-leaved Duckweed (*L. trisulca*) (illustrated left), with *stalked, translucent, ivy-like fronds*, often with *daughter plants attached*, floats just beneath the surface of a few ponds, mostly in C Scotland. Greater Duckweed (*Spirodela polyrhiza*), with *round fronds to 8 mm across* dangling *5-15 roots below*, is rare in the E.

Branched Bur-reed

Sparganium erectum
BUR-REED FAMILY

This *upright* perennial of still and slow-moving water and marshland, mostly in the S and E, has stiff stems to 1.5 m tall and *keeled, strap-shaped, sheathing leaves*, to 15 mm wide. Its *branched flower-spikes* in summer have *unstalked, rounded heads* of tiny, *3-6-lobed flowers*. The *smaller, upper heads are male* with *yellow stamens*, and the *broader female heads* below ripen into bur-like fruits.
Gael: Seisg Rìgh ('King's Sedge')

OTHER SPECIES: Unbranched Bur-reed (*S. emersum*), with *narrower, unkeeled leaves, unbranched inflorescences* and *stalked heads*, grows scattered in shallow water. Floating Bur-reed (*S. angustifolium*), with *long, floating stems* and *unbranched inflorescences with 2 male heads*, inhabits peaty pools in the NW. Least Bur-reed (*S. minimum*), *with shorter floating stems* and *a single male head*, is occasional in ponds and ditches.

Bulrush

Typha latifolia
REEDMACE FAMILY

Although not the true Bulrush of the Bible, the name has stuck to this robust perennial, also called Reedmace, of reed-swamps, lochs and riversides in the S and E. Its *strap-shaped, greyish-green leaves* overtop an *unbranched flower-stem*, to 2 m tall, with a *cylindrical, chocolate-brown spike* of female flowers, immediately beneath a narrower, *fluffy, straw-coloured male spike*, fertile in midsummer.

Gael: Cuigeal nam Ban-sìdh ('Fairy Women's Distaff')

A few remnants of native Scots Pine woodland still survive, as precious as any Cathedral, like this on the shores of Loch Rannoch in Perthshire

All around the Highlands and Islands, breathtaking scenery is guaranteed, but the flowers of the Highlands take a little more finding. Although many unusual and attractive species grow here, the cool and often wet climate and the generally poor soils mean that they are rarely abundant.

Many parts of the central Highlands are at their most colourful in late August and early September when Heather is in full bloom, transforming whole hillsides into glorious sheets of purple. But this spectacle is largely man-made. By nature, Heather is an understorey shrub of pine woodland, but almost all the native pinewoods of Scotland have long since been felled.

Where Heather is abundant today, it is maintained by careful moor-burning. This ensures a plentiful growth of young Heather shoots to feed Red Grouse, the gamebird that is shot for sport on Highland estates from the 'Glorious Twelfth' of August each year. The burning produces the characteristic patchwork-quilt appearance of many moors, amongst which Foxglove (p. 38) sometimes flowers abundantly. In older stands, a search beneath the Heather can sometimes reveal tiny, hidden plants of Lesser Twayblade orchid. Patches of purple on the hill earlier in the year are more likely to belong to Bell Heather, which is distinguished from Heather by its larger, richer-red flowers. It is a plant of drier peaty soils, replaced in boggier moorland by Cross-leaved Heath. Other members of the Heather family also grow on these moors. Bilberry (Blaeberry in Scots) prefers drier moors, where its deciduous leaves are often much-grazed by sheep. On slightly damper and more exposed moors, it is joined or replaced by the evergreen Cowberry (often, confusingly, called Cranberry in Scotland). In Speyside, Deeside and elsewhere in the north, Bearberry – another heath with evergreen leaves – is also locally abundant, sometimes tumbling like a curtain over recently-cut roadside banks.

Where some native pinewood does survive – most notably around Deeside and Speyside, near Loch

Many moors in eastern Scotland show this patchwork-quilt pattern when heather is burnt to encourage grouse for sport-shooting

One-flowered Wintergreen, growing here with Small Cow-wheat, is a rare evergreen of old-established pinewoods in the north-east Highlands. Photo by Ian Rose

Rannoch, in Glen Affric west of Inverness, and at Beinn Eighe in Wester Ross (see 'Places to Visit') – characteristic pinewood flowers also occur. The most widespread of these are Common, Intermediate and Serrated Wintergreen, the unrelated Chickweed Wintergreen (which also survives out onto open moorland) and Creeping Lady's-tresses orchid. All of these will also move into well-established pine plantations.

One-flowered Wintergreen (also called St Olaf's Candlestick) (*Moneses uniflora*), with thread-like stems and solitary, dropping, waxy-white flowers, about 15 mm across, is very much rarer in a few open, mossy pinewoods in the north-east. Equally uncommon in both pine and birch woods in the eastern Highlands is the delicate little Twinflower (*Linnaea borealis*). Its creeping stems and paired, nodding, pink, funnel-shaped flowers are perhaps sometimes overlooked.

Interspersed with the moors and woods, many lochs add reflected glory to the Highland landscape. Their cold, acid waters generally support few plants, but, in some, the leaves and flowers of White or Yellow Water-lilies may be seen floating on the surface. More occasionally, the delicate, purple flowers of Water Lobelia are held above the water surface on long stalks arising from a rosette of leaves in the mud below. In early summer some shallower lochs, pools and bogs are pink with the frilled flowers of Bogbean.

The high rainfall of the west Highlands (reaching 198 cm in some areas) may seem an inconvenience to visitors, but it is also an important part of the Highland scene, shaping and colouring the landscape. Wherever the rainfall exceeds about 140 cm, peat tends to accumulate in vast blankets. In these bogs, Cotton-grasses, Sundews, Butterwort, Lousewort, Bog Myrtle and the creeping stems of Bog Cranberry are the main flowering plants amongst the bog mosses (*Sphagnum* species).

The sweeping bogs of the great empty zone in Caithness and Sutherland called the Flow Country (from the

Twinflower is a delicate plant that grows, half-hidden, in the understorey of a few pine and birch woods in the Highlands.

Peaty areas high in the mountains typically are home to plants like these. The flowers are Dwarf Cornel, the crinkled, lobed leaves belong to the Cloudberry, the plant with the bluish, rounded leaves at the top of the picture is Bog Bilberry, and the narrow, pale green leaves, which are commonest in this picture, are those of Cowberry.

Norse word for a marshy moor) are the most special of all. Interspersed with an intricate pattern of pools, these are also the home for a number of arctic plants, including the dwarf species of birch (*Betula nana*), which rarely exceeds 50 cm in height and has rounded, toothed leaves. A Visitor Centre at Forsinard on the A897 road north of Helmsdale illustrates the international importance of this area, which is best seen from the railway line to Wick.

The cold winter weather in the far north-west reduces the growing season and helps to encourage an arctic-alpine flora, even at low altitudes. The richest displays occur where limestone outcrops near the surface, at Durness and Inchnadamph in Sutherland and around Torrin, west of Broadford on Skye, but similar conditions are also produced by shell-sand deposited by the wind on steep banks at the mouth of the Naver in Sutherland (see 'Places to Visit'). All these areas hold a superb flora, including many species which would require a high mountain climb to see elsewhere.

Although the mountain tops are beyond the scope of this book, there are some places where roads rise through high mountain passes and commoner arctic-alpine species are easily seen at the roadside. One of the best sites is around the ski area at Glenshee, south of Braemar (see 'Places to Visit'), although the ski road to Cairn Gorm, near Aviemore, also allows access to some commoner mountain plants. Arctic-alpines can also be seen beside the path to the Grey Mare's Tail in Dumfriesshire, on some of the more accessible walks in Glencoe, or beside the summit of the Bealach na Ba, the 'Pass of the Cattle' road to Applecross in Wester Ross. Sadly, however, some of the richest botanical sites are too sensitive to be publicised here; at some sites too many visitors' feet can do almost as much damage as too many grazing sheep or deer.

The Flow Country is a great 'empty area' of moorland and pools, with uncommon arctic plants, in the far north of Sutherland and Caithness

189

Climbing Corydalis

Ceratocapnos claviculata
FUMITORY FAMILY

Obviously related to the fumitories (p.44), this *slender, climbing annual* has *brittle, much branched stems*, 20-80 cm long, and *leaves divided into oval segments* and ending in a *twining tendril* by which the plant clambers over vegetation and walls. In summer it produces spikes of about 6 *tubular, creamy-white flowers*, 5-6 mm long, with a *short spur behind*. It grows in rocky, heathy, scrubby and wooded areas on acid soils, scattered around Scotland except the Isles.

Gael: Fliodh an Tughaidh ('Chickweed of the Thatch')

OTHER SPECIES: Yellow Corydalis (*Pseudofumaria lutea*), a *tufted perennial to 30 cm tall with dense spikes of 6-16 golden-yellow flowers*, is naturalised on old walls, mostly in the E.

Marsh Violet

Viola palustris
VIOLET FAMILY

This *hairless* violet has no *aerial stems* but a *creeping underground stem* which produces a tuft of *almost circular, wavy-edged leaves* with a *heart-shaped base* on *stalks to 4 cm long*, and, in spring and summer, *flowerstalks no longer than the leaves*. The *typical violet flowers* (p.65), 10-15 mm vertically, are *rather compressed laterally* with *pale-lilac* (*rarely white*), *darker-veined petals* and a *spur hardly longer than the backward-pointing flaps on the pointed sepals*. The plant grows in bogs and marshy ground throughout Scotland.

Gael: Dail-chuach Lèana ('Marsh Field Cup')

Heath Milkwort

Polygala serpyllifolia
MILKWORT FAMILY

The commoner of 2 near-identical milkworts, this slender perennial grows on heaths and lime-free grassland throughout Scotland. It is 10-30 cm tall, with *unstalked, narrowly oval leaves, the lowest of which are opposite* (although shed by late season, leaving *opposite leaf-scars*). In spring and summer, it has spikes of 3-10 flowers, 4-6 mm long, with *3 fused petals*, which are *usually gentian- or slate-blue* but often pink or white, and 5 *sepals*, the inner 2 of which are *larger, petal-coloured and enclose the flower.*
Gael: Siabann nam Ban-sìdh ('Fairy Women's Soap')

OTHER SPECIES: Common Milkwort (*P. vulgaris*), with only *alternate (not paired) leaves* and *spikes of 10-40 blue, pink or white flowers*, 4-7 mm long, is more scattered in lime-rich grassland.

Bog Stitchwort

Stellaria uliginosa
PINK FAMILY

Widespread throughout Scotland in wet, acid soils, Bog Stitchwort is a *straggling perennial* with *square, hairless stems* to 40 cm long, and opposite pairs of *bluish-green, unstalked, narrowly oval leaves*, 5-10 mm long. Its *flowers*, 4-6 mm across, have 5 *white petals cleft almost to the base*, and 5 *longer, narrow sepals*.
Gael: Flige ('Wetness')

OTHER SPECIES: Marsh Stitchwort (*S. palustris*), like Greater Stitchwort (p. 132) but with *narrower, smooth-edged leaves* and *petals divided to the base*, grows in a few S marshes.

191

Slender St. John's-wort

Hypericum pulchrum
ST. JOHN'S-WORT FAMILY

This elegant perennial has *slender, reddish stems*, 10-90 cm tall, which are *not ridged or winged* (cf species on p.66). Its *paired, broadly oval leaves*, 5-20 mm long, *half-clasp the stem* and are *dotted with translucent glands*. Its flowers in summer are about 15 mm across with 5 *reddish-tinged, yellow petals, dotted with black glands near their margins*, and 5 *much shorter sepals* also with *marginal black glands*. The plant grows in heathy and grassy places on acid soils throughout Scotland.
Gael: Lus Chaluim Chille ('St Columba's Plant')

Trailing St. John's-wort

Hypericum humifusum
ST. JOHN'S-WORT FAMILY

The *trailing, wiry stems*, to 30 cm long, of this *hairless* perennial are marked by *2 raised lines*. It has pairs of *unstalked, oblong leaves* to 15 mm long, usually with *black glands*, and clusters of a few flowers, 8-12 mm across, in summer. These have 5 yellow petals up to *twice as long* as the *black-dotted sepals*, which are *unequal in size*. The plant grows in scattered heaths and dry moors, but is absent from the Isles.
Gael: Beachnuadh Làir (derivation unclear; làir = ground)

OTHER SPECIES: Marsh St. John's-wort (*H. elodes*) with *creeping stems, grey-woolly, broadly oval leaves* and *pale-yellow, bell-shaped flowers*, forms mats in marshes and boggy pools in the far W and W islands.

192

Whin

Ulex europaeus
PEA FAMILY

'Officially' named Gorse, but generally called Whin in Scotland, this *evergreen shrub*, to 2 m tall, is *densely armed with rigid, grooved spines* to 25 mm long. It flowers sporadically through mild winters, and prolifically from early spring (see p. 6), with *golden-yellow, almond-scented pea-flowers* (see p.71), 11-20 mm long. These develop into *hairy brown pods* which explode audibly in dry weather, dispersing their poisonous seeds. Whin grows in rough grassy places on acid soils throughout Scotland, but is introduced on the N Isles.

Gael: *Conasg (derived from conas = quarrel or wrangle)*

OTHER SPECIES: Western Gorse (*U. gallii*), a shorter, *spreading shrub* with *slightly furrowed spines* and late summer flowers 10-13 mm long, is rare in heathland in the SW and E (cf Petty Whin overleaf).

Broom

Cytisus scoparius
PEA FAMILY

Broom differs from Whin in *lacking spines* and having *stalked, often hairy, 3-lobed leaves*, which are shed in winter. It stands to 2 m tall, with *green, strongly angled twigs*. In *early summer*, its *golden-yellow flowers*, to 2 cm long with *spirally-coiled styles*, grow in the angles of leaves. They ripen to *black pods*, 2.5-4 cm long, which have *grey marginal hairs* and explode when ripe. Broom grows in sandy heaths and lime-free woods and wasteground around Scotland, but is planted in the Isles.

Gael: *Bealaidh (derivation obscure)*

193

Petty Whin

Genista anglica
PEA FAMILY

This spiny shrub *rarely exceeds 50 cm tall*, with wiry, brown stems. Its *spines*, 1-2 cm long, *grow in the angles of narrow leaves* (distinguishing it from Whin and Western Gorse, p. 193), although occasional plants (illustrated) have spines absent. The non-spined leaves are *more oval and pointed*. Yellow flowers, 8-19 mm long with *the standard shorter than the keel* (see p.71), appear in early summer in leaf angles near the stem tips, ripening into *narrow, curved, hairless pods*. Petty Whin grows on dry heaths and moors in the Borders and C Highlands only.
Gael: Conasg Snàthadach ('Needle-like Whin')

New Zealand Willowherb

Epilobium brunnescens
WILLOWHERB FAMILY

Brought into gardens from New Zealand, this mat-forming perennial was first found in the wild in 1908 and is now surprisingly widespread in moist stony ground, especially in upland areas, scattered throughout Scotland including Orkney and the W Isles. It has *reddish, creeping stems* to 20 cm long, and *paired, oval, often bronze-coloured leaves*, 2.5-10 mm long. Its solitary, typical willowherb flowers (see p. 162) appear in leaf angles in summer and autumn *on stalks to 4 cm long* (longer in fruit). The *pale pink flowers*, 3-4 mm across, have *deeply-notched petals* and *shorter, often reddish sepals*.
Gael: Seileachan Làir ('Ground Willowherb')

194

Round-leaved Sundew

Drosera rotundifolia
SUNDEW FAMILY

Remarkable *carnivorous* plants of bogs and wet peaty places, sundews have *reddish leaf hairs* exuding dew-like drops of sweet juice which attract and briefly impede small insects. The leaf hairs then bend over, trapping the struggling insects, which are soon digested to provide nutrients. This is the commonest species, found in suitable habitats throughout Scotland. It has a rosette of *rounded leaves, 4-10 mm across, abruptly narrowed into a hairy stalk* to 3 cm long. Its flowers appear in summer on leafless stalks to 10 cm tall, but often remain closed, shedding their pollen internally. When they do open, they are about 6 mm across with usually 5 or 6 *white petals*.
Gael: *Lus na Feàrnaich* ('Plant of the Alder')

Great Sundew

Drosera longifolia
SUNDEW FAMILY

With similar carnivorous habits and flowers, this plant of *wetter bogs* in the W and N is distinguished by its *longer, narrower leaves*, with blades to 3 cm long, *gradually narrowed* into a *very long, hairless stalk*. Its flowerstalk, *up to 20 cm long,* emerges from the *centre of the leaf rosette*.
Gael: *Lus a' Ghadmainn* ('Plant of the Nit (Insect)')

OTHER SPECIES: Oblong-leaved Sundew (*D. intermedia*) has similar *oblong leaves* with *blades to 1 cm long,* and *flowerstalks to 10 cm tall* curving up from *beneath the leaf rosette*. It is rarer in damp, open peat in the W.

195

Bog Myrtle

Myrica gale
BOG MYRTLE FAMILY

Willow-like in general appearance, this shrub of bogs and wet heathland throughout the SW, Highlands and islands, except Shetland, is recognisable by the *resinous smell* of its crushed leaves. It spreads by suckers, forming stands of stems to 1.5 m tall, with *reddish-brown twigs*. The *catkins* appear on leafless twigs in spring, before the leaves develop, with the *reddish-brown male catkins, 7-15 mm long*, on separate plants from the *redder, 5-10 mm long female catkins*. The leaves, which develop later, are *greyish-green, narrowly oval, toothed near the tip*, and *hairy and dotted with yellow, resinous glands underneath*.
Gael: *Roid (derivation obscure)*
Bog Myrtle oil is being investigated for use as a midge repellent.

Bog Pimpernel

Anagallis tenella
PRIMROSE FAMILY

This delicate, *mat-forming, hairless* perennial has *creeping, rooting stems*, 5-20 cm long, with opposite pairs of *short-stalked, oval or almost circular leaves* to 1 cm long. Its single *flowers* are borne well above the leaves in summer on *slender stalks* emerging from leaf angles. The flowers have a *pale pink, funnel-shaped petal-tube*, with *5 darker-veined lobes* which spread out in sunshine to 14 mm across. The plant grows in bogs and damp peaty places, quite commonly in the W and W Isles, and more rarely in the E, NW and N Isles.
Gael: *Falcair Lèana ('Marsh Cleanser' cf p.120)*

196

HEATHERS

Members of the Heather family (such as Mountain Bearberry, right) are low-growing shrubs with undivided, deciduous or evergreen leaves. Their flowers, often in showy spikes or clusters, have 4-5 free or joined sepals, 4-5 petals united into a bell- or urn-shaped tube and twice as many stamens. Their fruits are berries or dry capsules. All grow in lime-free heathland, moorland or bogs, aided by nutrient-providing fungal partners in their roots, often becoming dominant over large areas.

Bearberry

Arctostaphylos uva-ursi
HEATHER FAMILY

A *mat-forming shrub* with *far-spreading, rooting branches* and *reddish young twigs*, Bearberry has *leathery, evergreen, untoothed, oval leaves*, which are *broadest near the tip, dark-green and glossy above* and *paler with a conspicuous network of veins underneath*. Its flowers, clustered at branch tips in early summer, are *urn-shaped*, contracted beneath their rim, 4-6 mm long, and *pale pink* with a *deeper rose rim*. They ripen into *glossy red berries*, inedible to humans but once favoured by bears. Bearberry grows in drier moors scattered through the Highlands and Isles (see p. 185), and is very rare in the Border hills.
Gael: Grainnseag ('Little Grainy One' ie 'Berry')

OTHER SPECIES: Mountain or Alpine Bearberry (*A. alpinus*) (illustrated in box above), with *thinner, paler green, wrinkled, toothed, deciduous leaves, white flowers* and *black berries*, is much rarer in rocky moors on the N mainland and Orkney.

Blaeberry

Vaccinium myrtilis
HEATHER FAMILY

Found in moors and open woods on acid soils throughout Scotland. Blaeberry (known as Bilberry in England) is the dominant plant in a zone above Heather in mountains. It stands to 60 cm tall, with *twisted, angled, green stems* and *thin, deciduous, bright-green, toothed, oval leaves,* 1-3 cm long. Its nodding flowers, single or paired in leaf angles in spring, are an *inflated globe shape,* to 6 mm long, *greenish-red,* with short, *curled-back lobes,* and develop into *edible bluish-black berries.*
Gael: Caora-mhitheag (Caora = 'berry'; mhitheag obscure)

Cowberry

Vaccinium vitis-idaea
HEATHER FAMILY

Often confusingly called Cranberry in Scotland, Cowberry is common in moors and woods on acid soils in the Highlands and Borders, and scattered on the islands. It has *unridged, brown stems,* to 30 cm tall, and *dark-green, leathery, evergreen leaves.* These resemble Bearberry leaves (p. 197), but are *broadest in the middle* with *inrolled margins* and *dark glands dotting the underside.* It has *pinkish-white, bell-shaped flowers,* around 6 mm long, with *4 curled-back petal-lobes,* in nodding groups of 2-4 in *midsummer,* and edible but bitter *red berries.*
Gael: Lus nam Braoileag ('Plant of the Berries')

OTHER SPECIES: Bog Rosemary (*Andromeda polifolia*), a low shrub with *narrow, shiny, grey-green leaves,* and *2-4 long-stalked, nodding, pink, urn-shaped flowers,* grows in a few bogs in C and S Scotland.

198

Bog Bilberry

Vaccinium uliginosum
HEATHER FAMILY

Often growing amongst Blaeberry carpets on deep peat, usually above 400 m altitude, Bog Bilberry is distinguished by its *brown, unridged stems*, to 50 cm tall, and its *thicker (but deciduous), untoothed, bluish-green leaves*. Its flowers, in nodding groups of *1-4 in leaf angles* in early summer, are *pale-pink and urn-shaped*, around 4 mm long, with *short, curled-back lobes*, ripening to edible *bluish-black berries*. It is a local plant of the C and W Highlands, Jura and the N Isles, and also occurs rarely in the Border hills.

Gael: Dearc Roide (perhaps 'Bitter Berry')

Cranberry

Vaccinium oxycoccus
HEATHER FAMILY

Not to be confused with the Scots name for Cowberry (opposite), this is a *creeping, evergreen undershrub* of bogs and wet moorland in C and S Scotland and the C Highlands, much rarer in the N. It has *thread-like stems* with *sparse, alternating, untoothed, oval leaves*, 4-8 mm long, and broadest near the middle. Its flowers are held erect in summer on *slender, downy stalks* to 3 cm long, and have *4 pink petal-lobes* which *curl back*, displaying a 'beak' of yellow stamens. Its *red berry* is edible.

Gael: Muileag ('Little Frog')

OTHER SPECIES: Small Cranberry (*V. microcarpum*) with *triangular leaves, broadest at their base, 3-5 mm long, and hairless flowerstalks*, is rarer in bogs in the C Highlands and Caithness.

199

Heather

Calluna vulgaris
HEATHER FAMILY

Also known as Ling, Heather grows naturally in pinewoods and a narrow zone above the treeline on mountains, and its dominance in moorland throughout Scotland today is encouraged by grouse management (see p. 184). It is a bushy shrub to 60 cm tall (or 1 m where unmanaged). Its twisting, *leafless stems* have *many short side shoots*, *packed with opposite rows of needle-shaped leaves*, to 2 mm long, with *bent-back margins*. Its flowers, in *crowded, leafy spikes*, have 4 sepal-like bracts, 4 *pinkish-purple sepal-lobes*, and a *shorter, pink, bell-shaped petal-tube*, and appear abundantly in August and September (see p. 8). They develop into *round, dry capsules*.
Gael: *Fraoch (derivation obscure)*

Bell Heather

Erica cinerea
HEATHER FAMILY

Almost as abundant as Heather in drier moorland throughout Scotland except for parts of the C belt, Bell Heather has *larger flowers*, with a *deeper reddish-purple, urn-shaped petal-tube*, 5-6 mm long, with 4 *short, curled-back lobes*, and 4 short, purple sepal-lobes. They appear from July, before Heather is in full bloom, in *whorled spikes to 7 cm long*, developing into *many-seeded dry capsules*. Bell Heather stands to 60 cm tall, with many ascending shrubby stems and *needle-shaped leaves* arranged in *whorls of 3* or *bunched into knot-like clusters*.
Gael: *Fraoch a' Bhadain ('Tufted Heather')*

200

Cross-leaved Heath

Erica tetralix
HEATHER FAMILY

Sometimes called Bog Heather, this *softly hairy, evergreen shrub*, to 60 cm tall, prefers wetter ground than Bell Heather in bogs and moorland over a similar range, although both grow together where soil dampness is variable. It has *greyish, hairy, needle-shaped leaves*, with *bent-down margins hiding the undersurface*, in *cross-like whorls of 4* up the stems. In summer, it has *compact, 1-sided clusters of 4-12 drooping flowers*. These have a *more inflated, paler pink petal-tube* than Bell Heather, and are 6-7 mm long, with short, hairy, grey-green sepal-lobes.
Gael: Fraoch Frangach ('French Heather')

Crowberry

Empetrum nigrum ·
CROWBERRY FAMILY

A *mat-forming shrub*, 15-45 cm tall, Crowberry grows in peaty and rocky moorland, mountain plateaux and clifftop heaths throughout Scotland. Its many stems are densely covered in *short-stalked, hairless, needle-shaped leaves*, 4-7 mm long. Its *tiny, easily-overlooked flowers*, 1-2 mm across with 6 *purplish lobes*, appear in the angles of stem-tip leaves in early summer. Male flowers (with 3 stamens) usually grow on separate plants from females. Pollen is spread by wind or rain splashes and the resulting fruit is a *round, black, bitter berry*. However, high mountain plants have bisexual flowers with stamens and ovaries, the stamens remaining as a tuft on the berries.
Gael: Lus na Feannag ('Crow's Plant')

Lousewort

Pedicularis sylvatica
FIGWORT FAMILY

Lousewort is a nearly hairless, *biennial or perennial* partial parasite (see p. 82) of damp heaths, bogs and marshes throughout Scotland. Its stem is *8-25 cm tall* with many *spreading branches*. Its often purplish *leaves* are *oblong in outline, up to 2 cm long*, and divided into many *narrow, deeply-toothed lobes*. In spring and summer it produces *leafy spikes of 3-10 flowers*. These have a *mostly hairless, cylindrical, 5-angled sepal-tube* with *4 leafy teeth*, and a *pink, red or rarely white, 2-lipped petal-tube, 20-25 mm long*. The *hooded upper lip* has *2 teeth near its tip* and the lower lip is *divided into 3 rounded lobes*.

Gael: Lus Riabhach Monaidh ('Brindled Plant of the Moor')

Marsh Lousewort

Pedicularis palustris
FIGWORT FAMILY

Also known as Red-rattle (from its dry rattling fruit capsules), this *annual to biennial* prefers rather wetter heaths and bogs and is a little less common than Lousewort over a similar range. It is *more erect-growing*, to 60 cm tall, with long, upright branches from the base of its purplish stem, giving it a *pyramidal shape*. Its leaves are *2-4 cm long, triangular in outline*, with *more deeply divided lobes*. Its flowers are similar, but with a *hairy, reddish, strongly 2-lipped sepal-tube* and with *5 teeth round the hooded tip of the upper petal lip*.

Gael: Lus Riabhach ('Brindled Plant')

Common Butterwort

Pinguicula vulgaris
BLADDERWORT FAMILY

This distinctive *carnivorous* plant grows in bogs, wet heaths and even on bare wet rocks throughout Scotland apart from some C areas. It has a basal rosette of *oblong, yellow-green leaves, 2-8 cm long*, with *inrolled margins* and covered in glistening *sticky glands* which trap and digest small insects for nourishment. 1 to several leafless, downy flowerstalks, *5-18 cm tall*, grow from the rosette in late spring and summer, topped by *solitary, 2-lipped, purple flowers*, 14-22 mm long, with a *slightly curved spur*, 3-6 mm long, behind. The *lower petal-lip is 3-lobed*, with the central lobe broadest and *paler near the throat*, and the upper lip has *2 backward-curved lobes*.
Gael: Mòthan ('Bog Violet')

Pale Butterwort

Pinguicula lusitanica
BLADDERWORT FAMILY

Much smaller and more delicate than the previous species, Pale Butterwort has a rosette of *olive-green leaves, 1-2 cm long* with reddish veins. It flowers from summer to early autumn on slender, downy, leafless flowerstalks, *3-10 cm tall*. Its petal-tube is *pinkish to pale lilac, 7-9 mm long*, with a *pale-yellow throat*, a *stubby, downward-curved spur, 2-4 mm long*, and *rounded, notched petal-lobes*. Because it overwinters as a rosette, it is frost-sensitive and so confined to the W, in bogs and wet moorland from Sutherland to Kintyre and Wigtownshire.
Gael: Mòthan Beag Bàn ('Little White Bog Violet')

203

Wood Sage

Teucrium scorodonia
THYME FAMILY

Wood Sage grows in dry, shady heathland and rocky places on lime-free soils throughout Scotland apart from Shetland and parts of the NE. Its stems, to 30 cm tall, have opposite pairs of *downy, wrinkled, heart-shaped leaves*, and are topped in summer by slender spikes of *greenish-yellow flowers*, 8-9 mm long, in the angles of short leafy bracts. The sepal-tube has *1 wide and 4 narrow teeth*, and the petal-tube has a *single, 5-lobed lip* with a *large middle lobe* and *4 protruding scarlet stamens*.

Gael: *Sàisde Coille (from English)*

Heath Bedstraw

Galium saxatile
BEDSTRAW FAMILY

This *slender, scrambling or mat-forming* bedstraw has *smooth, 4-angled stems* and whorls of 6-8 *bluntly oval leaves, broadest near the tip*, 7-10 mm long, and with *tiny, forward-pointing marginal prickles*. Its white bedstraw flowers (see p.40), 3 mm across, are clustered in summer on paired stalks, arising from leaf whorls and *shorter than the length of stem between leaf whorls*. The plant is abundant in heathland, woods and grassland on acid soils throughout Scotland.

Gael: *Màdar Fraoich ('Heather Madder')*

OTHER SPECIES: Limestone Bedstraw (G. *sterneri*), an uncommon plant of limestone grassland, has *narrower leaves, broadest just above the middle with backward-pointing marginal prickles*, and *flowerstalks longer than the length of stem between leaf whorls*.

204

Heath Cudweed

Gnaphalium sylvaticum
DAISY FAMILY

More erect than Marsh Cudweed (p.179), this *white-woolly perennial* grows on acid heaths and grassland around Scotland. It has flowering shoots to 60 cm tall, with *spear-shaped leaves*, 2-8 cm long, which are *green above and white-woolly beneath* and *become shorter up the stem*. In summer it has *long, leafy spikes* of *oblong, rayless daisy flowerheads*, around 6 mm long, cupped by bracts with *green centres and brown margins*.

Gael: Cnàmh-lus Mòintich ('Moorland Cud-weed')

OTHER SPECIES: Common Cudweed (*Filago vulgaris*), a grey woolly annual to 30 cm tall, with *wavy-edged, strap-shaped leaves*, 1-2 cm long, and *rounded clusters of 20-40 rayless yellow daisy flowerheads*, and Small Cudweed (*F. minima*), to 15 cm tall with *shorter leaves* and *clusters of 3-7 flowerheads*, are both uncommon, mostly in E heaths and roadsides.

Mountain Everlasting

Antennaria dioica
DAISY FAMILY

This *tufted* perennial of lime-rich grassland and heaths has rosettes of *spoon-shaped leaves*, 1-4 cm long, *white-woolly beneath*, and flowering stems to 20 cm tall with narrower leaves. Male and female flowers grow on separate plants in early summer in stem-tip clusters of 2-8. The *pink male flowerheads* (right illustration) are surrounded by *white, ray-like bracts*; the *rose-pink female flowerheads* (left) *lack bracts*.

Gael: Spòg Cait ('Cat's Paw')

MARSH ORCHIDS

Marsh Orchids (*Dactylorhiza* species), such as Common Spotted Orchid (right and p.97), are a complex group with 7 species and many subspecies in Scotland. They hybridise freely, adding to identification problems. They have a few strap-shaped, often dark-spotted leaves, not in an obvious rosette, and dense spikes of flowers. These usually have outer sepals and petals forming a hood, a 3-lobed lower lip marked with lines and dots, and a nectar-containing spur.

They propagate by root tubers spreading like fingers, unlike the 2 rounded root tubers of the genus *Orchis* commemorated in the Gaelic name for orchid – *Mogairlean* from *magairle* meaning a testicle.

Heath Spotted Orchid

Dactylorhiza maculata
ORCHID FAMILY

The commonest Scottish orchid, this grows throughout the country, sometimes abundantly, in acid moorland, marshes and open woodland. It rarely exceeds 30 cm tall, with up to 8 *strap-shaped leaves marked with pale purple blotches*, the lowest leaves sheathing the stem. It has a pyramidal head of 5-20 flowers in early summer. These are *white to pale lilac* with *deeper pink dots and lines on the lower lip* and a spur 3-7 mm long. They resemble the flowers of Common Spotted Orchid (p.97) but the *central lobe of the lower lip is much smaller than the rounded side lobes or reduced to a narrow tooth*.

Gael: Mogairlean Mòintich ('Spotted Orchid')

Early Marsh Orchid

Dactylorhiza incarnata
ORCHID FAMILY

This variable orchid, with 4 Scottish subspecies, is usually 7-20 cm tall, with 3-7 strap-shaped, *yellowish-green, keeled leaves*, the lower sheathing the stem. From late spring, it produces inflorescences of 10-40 flowers, variable from *flesh pink to deep magenta*. These have a *shallowly 3-lobed lower lip, bent back at the sides* and marked with *loops and dots*, and a *stout spur, 6-9 mm long*. The plant grows in marshes and damp grassland scattered over Scotland, with a crimson-flowered subspecies in sand-dunes (see p.99).

Gael: *Mogairlean Lèana ('Marsh Orchid')*

Northern Marsh Orchid

Dactylorhiza purpurella
ORCHID FAMILY

Almost as widespread as Heath Spotted Orchid, this species grows in wet grassland and marshes scattered throughout Scotland. It stands 10-30 cm tall with 5-6, *unmarked or purple-blotched, broadly strap-shaped leaves with hooded tips*, the lower sheathing the stem. Its inflorescences in early summer have 10-40 *deep reddish-purple flowers* with a *diamond-shaped or slightly 3-lobed lower lip*, marked with *irregular lines and spots*, and a *tapered spur, 6-9 mm long*.

Gael: *Mogairlean Purpaidh ('Purple Orchid')*

OTHER SPECIES: The other 3 purple-flowered species are very rare, tricky to identify and confined entirely to a few sites in the W.

Lesser Twayblade

Listera cordata
ORCHID FAMILY

Although this orchid sometimes grows on exposed moss patches, its typical habitat in the Highlands and islands and more rarely in the Border hills is well hidden beneath clumps of Heather, where it may be more frequent than realised. It resembles a small Common Twayblade (p.95), but has a slightly hairy, *reddish stem, 5-10 (or occasionally 20) cm tall*, with two opposite *heart-shaped leaves*, 1-2 cm long, about 1/3 of the way up the stem. It flowers in early summer (with withered flowers surviving well into the autumn), producing a spike of *3-15 tiny reddish-green flowers* with spreading sepals and upper petals and a *deeply-forked lower lip* to 4 mm long.

Gael: Dà-dhuilleach Monaidh ('Two-leaved Plant of the Moor')

Bog Orchid

Hammarbya paludosa
ORCHID FAMILY

This tiny orchid grows in the open in wet bogs, uncommonly through the Highlands, W Scotland and W islands, where its *overall yellow-green colour* hides it perfectly amongst bog mosses. It is *2-10 cm tall*, with *2-3 oval leaves* to 1 cm long low on the stem, often fringed with minute bulbils which detach forming new plants. Its inflorescence in late summer has up to *20 flowers, about 5 mm long*. These are twisted so that the *striped green lip*, which is smaller than the spreading petals and sepals, is *at the top of the flower* (see illustration).

Gael: Mogairlean Bogaich (as English)

Frog Orchid

Coeloglossum viride
ORCHID FAMILY

Frog Orchid grows very locally in short grassland scattered around Scotland, including the Isles. Generally 10-20 cm tall, it can be shorter on windswept clifftops or taller on sheltered mountain ledges. Its stem has a *cluster of 2-5 oval leaves* sheathing its base with 1-3 narrower leaves further up the stem, and a cylindrical spike of 5-25 *green or red-tinged flowers* at the top of the stem in summer. These have a *loose hood of sepals and petals*, a *strap-shaped lower lip* to 6 mm long, divided at its base into *2 oblong outer lobes and a shorter middle lobe*, and a *stumpy spur*.
Gael: Mogairlean Losgainn (as English)

Bog Asphodel

Narthecium ossifragum
LILY FAMILY

In spring, the creeping underground stems of Bog Asphodel produce tufts of *rigid, strap-like basal leaves*, spreading in one plane, which lengthen to 5-30 cm. A longer flowering stem then develops, with a few short, sheathing leaves, and this is topped in midsummer by a *dense spike* of 6-20 flowers with *2 whorls of 3 narrow, yellow, petal-like lobes*, spreading to 15 mm across, and *6 orange stamens*. The *orange, spindle-shaped fruit capsule* remains on twiggy stems through the winter after shedding its seeds. The plant grows in bogs and wet moors, often abundantly, in all of Scotland, except for parts of the SE.
Gael: Bliochan ('Milk Plant', from bliochd = milk)

209

Common Cottongrass

Eriophorum angustifolium
SEDGE FAMILY

Although sedges are otherwise excluded from this book, this is such a conspicuous plant of wet moorland, bogs and bog pools throughout Scotland that it cannot be omitted. Its far-creeping underground stems produce patches of grass-like leaves, 3-6 mm wide, narrowed to a *long, 3-sided point* and turning red from the tip. The flower stems, 20-60 cm tall, end in early summer in a cluster of 3-7 *dropping heads* of inconspicuous, brownish-green flowers, *overtopped by a long sheathing bract*. By midsummer, the heads develop into *shining white balls* of long, cottony hairs on the fruits.
Gael: Canach (obscure; first element may mean 'white')

OTHER SPECIES: Broad-leaved Cottongrass (*E. latifolium*), with *apple-green leaves* ending in a *short 3-sided point*, grows in a few lime-rich bogs.

Harestail Cottongrass

Eriophorum vaginatum
SEDGE FAMILY

A plant of slightly less wet peatlands, especially blanket bogs, throughout Scotland, Harestail grows to 60 cm tall, with *tussocks* of narrow leaves *to 1 mm wide*. The stem is *sheathed by 2-3 inflated leaves* and topped in *spring* by a *solitary, egg-shaped head* of yellowish flowers, without bracts below. These develop by *early summer* to a *dense, fluffy white head*.
Gael: Sìoda Monaidh ('Mountain Silk')

White Waterlily

Nymphaea alba
WATERLILY FAMILY

This showy perennial grows, sometimes abundantly, at depths of 0.5-3 m in nutrient-poor lochs and ponds around Scotland except Orkney, but most commonly in the NW. Its *round, floating leaves* are 10-30 cm across, deeply notched where the stalk attaches and reddish underneath. The *floating flowers* in summer are 10-20 cm across, with 3-5 sepals, which are white above and olive-green beneath, 20-25 *large, white or pink-tinged petals* and a mass of stamens. Small-flowered plants in the NW and Isles belong to subspecies *occidentalis*.
Gael: *Duilleag-bhàite Bhàn* ('White Drowned Leaf')

Yellow Waterlily

Nuphar lutea
WATERLILY FAMILY

This species grows, less commonly, in lochs and ponds to 2 m deep, mainly in lowland areas. It has *deeply-notched, oval floating leaves* to *40 cm long*, with a few thin submerged leaves. Its flowers, *held above the water* on thick stalks in summer, are formed by *4-6 yellowish-green, overlapping sepals*, spreading to 4-6 cm across. Many *short yellow petals* and stamens are tucked inside the flower, around a *flask-shaped* ovary topped by a ring of stigma rays.
Gael: *Duilleag-bhàite Bhuidhe* ('Yellow Drowned Leaf')

OTHER SPECIES: Least Waterlily (*N. pumila*), with *leaves to 14 cm across* and *smaller flowers with 4-5 scarcely touching yellow sepals*, grows in a few Highland lochs.

211

Bogbean

Menyanthes trifoliata
BOGBEAN FAMILY

This handsome plant forms floating mats in ponds and shallow loch edges or creeps through wet bogs throughout Scotland but most commonly in the W. Its *leaves*, raised above the water surface on long stalks, have *3 oval, untoothed leaflets*. Its branching spikes of 10-20 flowers in early summer are held above the water on stalks to 30 cm tall. The *funnel-shaped flowers*, 15-20 mm across, have 5 sepal-lobes, and 5 *down-curved petal-lobes* which are *pink on the outside and paler on the inside with a fringe of white hairs guarding the throat* (so that only long-tongued bees or butterflies can pollinate it). The fruit is a *green, bean-shaped capsule*.
Gael: *Trì-bhileach* ('Three-lipped' or 'Three-leaved')

Shoreweed

Littorella uniflora
PLANTAIN FAMILY

Shoreweed spreads by rooting runners over the sandy or gravelly beds of lochs and reservoirs, scattered throughout Scotland, in water to 4 m deep and is only easily seen on shores when water levels are low in dry summers. It has tufts of *fleshy, half-cylindrical leaves*, 2-10 cm long, and tiny, green flowers which only develop where the plant is exposed in summer. The *short-stalked male flowers* are 5-6 mm across with *4 petals and 4 thread-like stamens to 2 cm long*. At the base of their stalks is a cluster of 2-8 *unstalked female flowers*, with *2-4 petals* and a style to 1 cm long.
Gael: *Lus Bòrd an Locha* ('Loch Shore Plant')

Lesser Bladderwort

Utricularia minor
BLADDERWORT FAMILY

Bladderworts are carnivorous aquatic plants which trap water organisms in *bladders* developed from their leaves. This is the commonest of several similar Scottish species, distinguished mainly by flower shape. It grows in ponds, ditches and bog-pools, mostly in the W, and has *2 different types of stems*. Some have *feathery green leaves* and few 2 mm-long bladders, and float freely; others, with *colourless, reduced leaves* and more bladders, are partly buried in the mud. It flowers sporadically in summer, with *2-6 yellow flowers*, 6-8 mm long, held above the water on a leafless stalk. The flowers have a *short spur* and *2-lipped sepal- and petal-tubes*, with the lower petal lip broader than the upper and swollen near the throat.

Gael: Lus nam Balgan Beag ('Small Bladder Plant')

Water Lobelia

Lobelia dortmanna
BELLFLOWER FAMILY

Growing to 3 m deep on the stony beds of acid lochs, Water Lobelia is confined to the SW, Highlands and islands. Its *strap-shaped leaves*, in a *submerged rosette*, are up to 4 cm long with *2 hollow tubes*, visible when the leaf is cut or broken open. Its *leafless flower-stem*, to 60 cm tall, holds a few *nodding, pale-lilac flowers* well above the water in late summer. These have a *5-toothed sepal-tube* and *2-lipped petal-tube*, the upper lip with *2, swept-back lobes* and the lower narrowly 3-lobed.

Gael: Flùr an Lochain ('Flower of the Lochan (small loch)')

213

Wood Vetch

Vicia sylvatica
PEA FAMILY

This attractive vetch has scrambling stems to 2 m long (usually less) and *leaves with 5-12 pairs of oblong leaflets, ending in a short point, and much-branched tendrils*. In early summer it produces *long-stalked, one-sided inflorescences* of 6-20 pea flowers (see p.71) to 2 cm long, which are *white with blue or purple veins* and ripen to *black, hairless pods*. It is uncommon in overgrown rocky places, screes, mountain woods and sea cliffs, scattered throughout the mainland and W islands.

Gael: Peasair Coille ('Wood Pea')

Round-leaved Wintergreen

Pyrola rotundifolia
WINTERGREEN FAMILY

Wintergreens are *evergreen* perennials (hence their name) which depend partly on a root fungus for nourishment. This species has a *basal rosette* of glossy, *slightly-toothed, almost circular leaves* with *stalks longer than blades*. Its leafless flowering stems, to 40 cm tall, are topped in late summer by a *loose spike* of open *bell-shaped flowers*, about 12 mm across, with 5 *white petals* and an *S-shaped style to 10 mm long*. It grows uncommonly in damp woodland, bogs and mountain cliff-ledges scattered in the S Highlands and Orkney.

Gael: Glas-luibh Cruinn ('Round Green Plant')

OTHER SPECIES: One-flowered Wintergreen (*Moneses uniflora*) (see p. 186), is very rare (and legally protected) in NE pinewoods.

Common Wintergreen

Pyrola minor
WINTERGREEN FAMILY

Much commoner than the preceding species, this grows in pine and birch woods, open moorland, damp rock-ledges and coastal dunes, scattered around the mainland and inner islands. Its *slightly-toothed, broadly oval leaves* grow low on the stem (not all basally) and have *stalks shorter than their blades*. Its flowers, in *denser spikes* on stems to 30 cm tall from early summer, are *white or pinkish, globe-shaped, about 6 mm across* and *completely enclose a 1-2 mm long style*.
Gael: Glas-luibh Beag ('Small Green Plant')

OTHER SPECIES: Intermediate Wintergreen (*P. intermedia*) of pinewoods and moors has *leaf-stalks equalling blades*, and *open globe-shaped flowers, 10 mm across*, with a *5 mm long style* just protruding.

Serrated Wintergreen

Orthilia secunda
WINTERGREEN FAMILY

A plant of upland woods and damp mountain rock-ledges in Highland and Border hills, Serrated Wintergreen is distinguished by its *well-toothed, light-green, pointed oval leaves*, 2-4 cm long, low on the stem, with *stalks shorter than their blades*, and its *dense, one-sided inflorescence* of *nodding, greenish-white flowers* in midsummer. These are *bell-shaped, about 5 mm across*, with a *straight, protruding style* about 5 mm long.
Gael: Glas-luibh Fiaclach ('Serrated Green Plant')

Chickweed Wintergreen

Trientalis europaea
PRIMROSE FAMILY

Neither a chickweed nor a wintergreen but a relative of primroses, this delicate plant spreads by creeping underground stems. Its slender aerial stems are 10-25 cm tall, bearing near the top a *whorl of 5-6 unequally-sized, stiff, shining, sometimes finely-toothed, oval leaves*, 1-8 cm long, with a few, small, alternating leaves lower down the stem. In summer it has *usually solitary flowers*, 15-18 mm across, with 5-9 (*typically 7*) *white petal-lobes*. It is locally common in pinewoods, including old plantations, and open, mossy moors to altitudes of 1000 m, often growing with Blaeberry, scattered through the Highlands and N Isles and less commonly in S hills.
Gael: Reul na Coille ('Star of the Wood')

Small Cow-wheat

Melampyrum sylvaticum
FIGWORT FAMILY

Very much a slender version of Common Cow-wheat (p. 142), Small Cow-wheat is distinguished by its *much narrower leaves* (no more than 12 mm wide) and pairs of *smaller, deeper yellow, 2-lipped flowers* in summer. These have a *petal-tube 6-10 mm long, scarcely exceeding the sepal-tube* which has *spreading teeth* (not pressed against the petal-tube as in Common Cow-wheat). The *3-lobed lower petal-lip is strongly bent down* (see flower detail). The plant grows in a few rocky mountain woods in the C Highlands, at altitudes of 200-400 m.
Gael: Càraid Bhuidhe Bheag ('Little Yellow Twins/Couple')

Creeping Lady's-tresses

Goodyera repens
ORCHID FAMILY

Typically a plant of native pine (or rarely birch) woods in the NE, this slender orchid has also established in old pine plantations in the Borders and elsewhere. It stands 8-35 cm tall, with a *basal rosette of 3-5 stalked, broadly oval, prominently 5-veined, evergreen leaves, 15-25 mm long,* and a *few short leaves clasping the stem*. In late summer it has a *spirally-twisted inflorescence* (like plaited hair) of *5-25 creamy-white* flowers with *2 spreading side lobes, a short hood* and a *narrow lower lip shorter than the side lobes*.

Gael: *Mogairlean Ealaidheach ('Creeping Orchid')*

Coral-root Orchid

Corallorhiza trifida
ORCHID FAMILY

The scientific and common names of this plant record its fleshy, coral-like underground stems, but destructive digging is not necessary for its identification and should always be avoided. It is a *pale-green saprophyte* (ie it relies on a fungal partner in its roots to obtain food from leaf litter). Its slender stems, *6-30 cm* tall, have *2-4, sheathing, scale-leaves*, and are topped in summer by a short spike of *4-13 nodding, greenish flowers*. These have *2 strap-shaped, red-tinged side lobes, a short hood* and a *white, shallowly 3-lobed, purple-spotted lower lip*. It grows in pine and birch woodland, boggy woodland by lochs and mires, and wet sand-dune hollows in the E and SW.

Gael: *Freumh Corail (from English)*

217

Alpine Meadow-rue

Thalictrum alpinum
BUTTERCUP FAMILY

This inconspicuous mountain perennial resembles Lesser Meadow-rue (p.116), but has an *unbranched inflorescence* in early summer of tiny flowers with 4 *pale-purple lobes* and a hanging tassel of 10-20 *violet stamens* with yellow anthers. It has wiry stems, 8-15 cm tall, and *glossy, dark-green leaves*, twice-divided into 9 leaflets which are roundish and shallowly-lobed. It grows in wet, gravelly flushes, damp mountain turf and rock ledges, throughout the Highlands and islands, from 1200 m altitude down to sea-level in the NW, with a few sites also in the Borders hills.

Gael: Rù Ailpeach ('Alpine Rue')

Mountain Pansy

Viola lutea
VIOLET FAMILY

Like a small Garden Pansy, this handsome plant grows in hill pastures in the S Highlands and hills of S Scotland, usually at altitudes of 200-600 m (but up to 1000 m). Its showy summer *flowers, 20-35 mm long vertically*, are generally *yellow* at low altitudes and S sites, and *red- or blue-violet with yellow at the base of the lower petal* at higher altitudes. Their *narrow spur* is 4 times as long as the sepal-flaps (cf Wild Pansy, p.65). The plant has slender, flexuous stems, 7-20 cm tall, and *bluntly oval leaves, narrowing up the stem*, with *finely-lobed, leaf-like appendages* (stipules) at their base.

Gael: Sàil-chuach an t-Slèibhe ('Mountain Heel Cup')

Moss Campion

Silene acaulis
PINK FAMILY

Out of flower, Moss Campion's low, compact, domed cushions of *narrow, bright-green leaves*, 6-12 mm long, look distinctly moss-like, but in midsummer the plant bursts into bloom. The *deep-rose (or rarely white) flowers*, to 12 mm across, hug the cushion on short stalks, and have *bell-shaped, reddish sepal-tubes with 5 blunt teeth* and longer, *shallowly notched petal-lobes*. The plant is confined to mountain grassland, cliffs and summit gravels to altitudes of 1280 m in the C and W Highlands and islands, but also occurs in exposed grassland down to sea-level in the W and the N Isles.

Gael: Coirean Còinnich ('Little Moss Cauldron')

Purple Oxytropis

Oxytropis halleri
PEA FAMILY

Reminiscent of Purple Milk-vetch (p.117), this *montane or N species* has *more silkily hairy leaves to 10 cm long*, with 10-14 pairs of narrow leaflets, and a *flower keel (see p. 71) ending in a sharp (often deeper purple) point*. It flowers in early summer, with hairy flowerstalks and *dense, rounded heads*, about 3 cm across, of 5-15 *blue-purple pea flowers*, 15-20 mm long. The plant is locally common in dunes and sand-blown hillsides on the N coast, and much rarer on sea-cliffs in E Ross and a few base-rich mountain cliffs, to above 600 m altitude, in the C and W Highlands.

Gael: Ogsatropas Corcarach (from English)

Cloudberry

Rubus chamaemorus
ROSE FAMILY

The *crinkled, glossy, lobed leaves* of this *creeping* perennial form open patches on the *deep peat* of mountain slopes and blanket bogs in the Highlands, and, less commonly, in the S Uplands and on Orkney. Its *solitary flowers*, in summer, are 15-20 mm across on stems 5-20 cm tall, with *5 white petals*, which soon fall, leaving *5 reddish sepals and many anthers*. The sweet, edible berries ripen from red to orange when ripe.

Gael: *Lus nan Oighreag* (derivation obscure)

OTHER SPECIES: Stone Bramble (*R. saxatilis*), with *rooting, above-ground runners* and *narrow-petalled, dirty-white flowers* to 10 mm across, grows amongst shady rocks in the Highlands, islands and S Uplands.

Mountain Avens

Dryas octopetala
ROSE FAMILY

This beautiful *creeping shrub* forms dense patches of *glossy, dark-green, deeply-veined leaves, lobed like oak leaves*, paler underneath and 5-20 mm long. Its flowers, in early summer on hairy stalks to 8 cm tall, are 25-40 mm across with *usually 8 (but occasionally 7-10) white petals* and numerous yellow stamens, ripening to a spirally twisted head of feathery hairs attached to dry fruits. It grows in base-rich grassland in C Highland mountains, on cliffs and grassy banks in Kintyre and on several W islands, and, most abundantly, in rich heathland near sea-level in the NW.

Gael: *Machall Monaidh* (perhaps 'Large-flowered Mountain Plant')

Alpine Lady's-mantle

Alchemilla alpina
ROSE FAMILY

Although obviously related to Common Lady's-mantle (p.75), this plant of mountain pastures and screes is distinguishable by its leaves, which are *divided almost to the base into 5-7 oblong, toothed lobes*, spreading like fingers and *densely covered underneath in silky hairs*, which show as a silvery rim round the lobes. Its yellow-green flowers in summer are *3 mm across*, in dense clusters at the tip of stems to 20 cm tall. The plant grows only in the Highlands, W islands and Shetland, usually at altitudes of 400-1200 m.

Gael: Trusgan ('Mantle') or Meangan Moire ('Mary's Twig')

Dwarf Cornel

Cornus suecica
DOGWOOD FAMILY

Improbably, this low-growing herb is a relative of Dogwood, a shrub to 4 m tall. It overwinters by a creeping underground stem from which aerial stems, 6-20 cm tall, develop each spring. These have *opposite pairs of almost stalkless, oval leaves*, 1-3 cm long, with *3-5 prominent veins* and a mat of hairs above. The apparent 'petals' in late summer are *white bracts* beneath a cluster of *8-25 tiny, dark-purple flowers*. These ripen to a cluster of *round, red berries*. The plant grows on mountain moors at altitudes of 200-900 m, widely in the C and W Highlands and more rarely in the S Uplands and N Isles.

Gael: Lus a' Chraois ('Wide-mouthed Plant')

Starry Saxifrage

Saxifraga stellaris
SAXIFRAGE FAMILY

This typical saxifrage has *basal rosettes* of *oblong, toothed, short-stalked leaves*, 5-30 mm long, and *leafless, sparsely-hairy flower-stems* to 20 cm tall. Its flowers, in an open inflorescence in summer, are 10-15 mm across with 5 sepals, 5 *narrow, white petals marked with 2 yellow basal spots* and 10 stamens. It grows by streams and in wet stony ground in mountains throughout the Highlands, in the S Uplands, and on islands including Orkney.

Gael: Clach-bhriseach Reultach ('Starry Stone-breaker')

OTHER SPECIES: Alpine Saxifrage (*S. nivalis*), with rather thick *leaves, purple beneath*, and *congested heads of smaller, unspotted white flowers*, 5-6 mm across, is rarer on rocks in the Highlands and S Uplands.

Purple Saxifrage

Saxifraga oppositifolia
SAXIFRAGE FAMILY

Flowering profusely *in early spring* as soon as the snows melt, this *creeping mat-former* also produces occasional flowers in midsummer. Then it is instantly recognisable, since it is the only Scottish saxifrage with *rosy-purple flowers*, 10-20 mm across. The trailing non-flowering stems are also distinctive, with opposite pairs of *unstalked, thick, bluish-green, oval leaves* densely packed on *red stems*. The plant grows on damp stony and rocky ground on mountains in the Highlands, W islands, N Isles and S Uplands from near sea-level in the NW to altitudes of 1215 m.

Gael: Clach-bhriseach Purpaidh ('Purple Stone-breaker')

Yellow Saxifrage

Saxifraga aizoides
SAXIFRAGE FAMILY

Saxifrage means 'rock-breaker', and this species can grow from bare rock where a runnel brings it moisture and nutrients. It forms patches of sprawling stems covered in *stalkless, slightly toothed, narrowly oblong leaves*, 1-2 cm long, with flowering stems to 20 cm tall. In summer, these are topped by an inflorescence of 1-10 flowers, 8-12 mm across, with *5 narrow, often red-spotted, yellow petals*. The plant grows in wet stony ground in mountains (see p. 236) in the Highlands, inner islands and Orkney, descending to near sea-level in the NW.

Gael: *Clach-bhriseach Buidhe* ('*Yellow Stone-breaker*')

Mossy Saxifrage

Saxifraga hypnoides
SAXIFRAGE FAMILY

The trailing stems of this species produce *moss-like mats of narrow, unlobed, pale-green leaves*, with central rosettes of *3-5-lobed leaves*. Arising from the rosettes are flower-stems to 20 cm tall with a few narrow, unlobed leaves and topped in early summer by *heads of 1-5 white flowers*, 14-20 mm across. The plant grows in mountain grassland and screes around the Highlands, S Uplands and inner islands.

Gael: *Clach-bhriseach Còinnich* ('*Mossy Stone-breaker*')

OTHER SPECIES: Rue-leaved Saxifrage, a delicate, *white-flowered annual* with *reddish, hairy stems* and *fleshy, 3- or 5-lobed leaves*, is uncommon in lime-rich grassland and on old walls in lowland areas.

223

Spignel

Meum athamanticum
CARROT FAMILY

Sometimes known as Baldmoney (the derivation of which is obscure), this *aromatic perennial* has *brown fibrous tufts* of old leaf sheaths at its stem base. Its leaves, mostly in an upright basal clump, are oval in outline and *finely divided into thread-like lobes*. Its *hollow stems*, to 60 cm tall, have a few, feathery, sheathing leaves and are topped in early summer by open umbels (see p.30), with *6-15 rays* and *frothy heads of white or pink-tinged flowers*, which develop into *ridged, egg-shaped fruits*, 7 mm long. The plant grows uncommonly in upland grassland in the S Highlands and SW Scotland.
Gael: Muilceann ('Aromatic Head' or possibly 'Bald Head')

Alpine Bistort

Persicaria vivipara
KNOTWEED FAMILY

Clearly related to Redshank (p.54), this is a showier plant to 30 cm tall. Its *lance-shaped leaves*, 2-7 cm long, are *dark-green above and bluish-green beneath*, with margins rolled under. The top of the inflorescence in summer is a spike of *white or pale pink flowers*, about 5 mm across, while the lower portion (or sometimes the entire inflorescence) is covered in *reddish-purple bulbils*, about 4 mm long, which drop off to form new plants or occasionally sprout while attached. Alpine Bistort grows in grassland and wet gravels in mountain areas, scattered through the Highlands and islands and more locally in the S Uplands.
Gael: Biolur Ailpeach (as English; Biolur cf Biolair, p. 156)

224

Mountain Sorrel

Oxyria digyna
DOCK FAMILY

This *fleshy docken* (see p.34) has *thick, long-stalked, kidney-shaped, leaves* to 3 cm long, mostly in *basal rosettes*. Its stems are 5-30 cm tall, topped by *branched, leafless spikes* of flowers with *4 sepal-like lobes*, the inner of which enlarge around the fruits. These consist of a nut, 3-4 mm long, with a *broad, green, often red-edged wing*. Mountain Sorrel grows on damp screes, ledges and streamsides in mountains to altitudes of over 1200 m in the Highlands, islands and S Uplands, but is often washed onto river shingle downstream.

Gael: Sealbhag nam Fiadh ('Deer Sorrel' — see p.77)

Dwarf Willow

Salix herbacea
WILLOW FAMILY

Although shrubby willows are beyond the scope of this book, this low-growing perennial frequently conceals its shrubby nature by keeping its woody stems underground, with only *low tufts of leaves* above ground. The leaves are *rounded, shining dark-green, net-veined, toothed* and 5-20 mm long. Tucked amongst them in midsummer are *shorter, yellow or reddish catkins* of 2-12 flowers. The male flowers, with red anthers, grow on separate plants from the females, which develop into *red pods*. Dwarf Willow grows on exposed mountain summits and ridges, usually above 600 m, in the Highlands, islands and S Uplands.

Gael: Seileach Ailpeach ('Alpine Willow')

OTHER SPECIES: Creeping Willow (*S. repens*), with *creeping stems* and *narrow leaves, silky hairy beneath*, grows in bogs and wet grassland.

Trailing Azalea

Loiseleuria procumbens
HEATHER FAMILY

One of the most beautiful mountain plants, this *trailing evergreen shrub*, related to Rhododendrons, grows on exposed moors and rocky mountain ridges, often where snow lies late, in the C and W Highlands, Skye and the N Isles, to altitudes of over 1200 m. Its stems are covered with *opposite pairs* of *shiny, dark-green, leathery, oblong leaves*, 3-8 mm long. Its flowers, in small groups raised little above the foliage in early summer, vary in abundance with spring weather. They have a *short, reddish, lobed sepal-tube*, and *5 deep-pink petals*, joined at the base into a *bell-shaped tube* but spreading above to 5 mm across. By midsummer, the flowers are replaced by *red, egg-shaped fruit capsules*.

Gael: *Lusan Albannach* ('Little Scottish Plant')

Northern Bedstraw

Galium boreale
BEDSTRAW FAMILY

The *only white-flowered bedstraw with leaves in whorls of 4* (cf. p.40), this rather stiff, rigid perennial has *4-angled stems* to 45 cm tall, and *widely-spaced whorls* of *dark-green, lance-shaped, 3-veined leaves*, 1-4 cm long with *rough margins*. Its *white flowers*, in a *pyramidal, leafy inflorescence* in midsummer, are 3 mm across, with *4 pointed petal-lobes*. They ripen to *olive-brown fruits covered in hooked bristles*. The plant grows on mountain cliffs and screes, to over 1000 m, in the S Uplands, Highlands and inner W islands only.

Gael: *Màdar Cruaidh* ('Hard Madder')

Dwarf Cudweed

Gnaphalium supinum
DAISY FAMILY

Like a stunted Marsh Cudweed (p.179), this *tufted perennial* has many leafy, non-flowering shoots and a few ascending flowering shoots, *rarely more than 6 cm tall*, with *narrow, white-woolly leaves*, 5-15 mm long. In midsummer, it produces *compact spikes* of 1-7 flowerheads, often with a group of broader leaves immediately beneath. The flowerheads are about 6 mm long, enclosed by a *cup of bracts with olive central strips and brown papery margins*. The plant grows on windswept shoulders and bare patches where snow lies late, usually above 500 m, in the Highlands and Skye only.

Gael: *Cnàmh-lus Beag* ('Small Plant that Wastes/Chews Slowly')

Scottish Asphodel

Tofieldia pusilla
LILY FAMILY

This delicate perennial, like a small Bog Asphodel (p.209) with *greenish-white flowers*, is not exclusively Scottish, despite its name, but is best seen in *base-rich* mountain springs and flushes at altitudes of 200-900 m, scattered across the Highlands and on Skye and Rum. It stands to 20 cm tall, with a *fan of stiff, sword-shaped leaves*, 15-40 mm long, and much smaller or no stem leaves. The flowers are packed in summer into dense, pyramidal heads, to 15 mm long, of 5-10 flowers with 6 *incurved, petal-like lobes* spreading to about 5 mm across. They ripen to *round green capsules*.

Gael: *Bliochan Albannach* ('Little Scottish Milk Plant'; cf p.209)

227

PLACES
TO VISIT

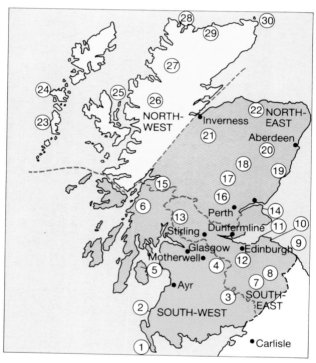

The sites which follow have been selected to show some of Scotland's most attractive and special wild flowers. They cover a diverse range of habitats, spread across Scotland, especially in areas likely to attract visitors for other reasons such as spectacular scenery. At some sites access is limited, so follow the instructions and the Botanical Code of Conduct (p. 13), respect other

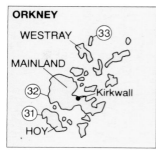

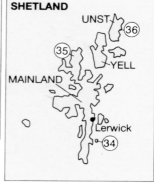

wildlife of the area, especially breeding birds, and always leave the flowers for later visitors to enjoy. May to July is generally the best time to visit. Many of the sites are nature reserves and some offer additional facilities noted in the text.

The areas follow (pre-1996) local government regions (see maps) and sites within each area are arranged roughly from the south-west corner. As well as standard abbreviations for directions, the following abbreviations are used:-

NNR = National Nature Reserve (managed by Scottish Natural Heritage, SNH – see pp. 248-9).

NTS = National Trust for Scotland

RSPB = Royal Society for the Protection of Birds

SWT = Scottish Wildlife Trust

To convert distances quoted, note that 1 mile = 1.6 kilometres.

Further details of many of the sites listed are available from local Tourist Information Centres. Ordnance Survey Landranger (1:50,000) maps are strongly recommended to find and explore the sites.

SOUTH-WEST SCOTLAND

The rugged seacliffs at The Mull of Galloway are home to a number of unusual flowers including this Rock Sea-spurrey

1. Mull of Galloway, Wigtownshire

RSPB reserve. 22 miles S of Stranraer. Follow A716 and B7065 onto minor road to lighthouse; car park before lighthouse entrance. KEEP BACK FROM DANGEROUS CLIFF EDGE.

These rugged cliffs support an interesting flora. Spring Squill and Purple Milk-vetch grow abundantly in the clifftop turf. Scots Lovage (at its southernmost British site), Roseroot, Golden Samphire (*Inula crithmoides*) and Rock Samphire (*Crithmum maritimum*) grow on the cliffs (best seen with binoculars!) near nesting seabirds.

2. Ballantrae Shingle Beach, Ayrshire

SWT reserve. Car park signed from the middle of Ballantrae village on the A77 S of Girvan; walk S along shore towards mouth of River Stinchar. KEEP OUT OF FENCED AREAS (BREEDING TERNS).

One of the few Scottish shingle spits (narrow promontories of accumulated stones), this has common sea-shore species such as Sea Campion, Thrift, Sea Plantain, Common Scurvy-grass and Sea Mayweed, as well as the rarer Oysterplant.

3. Grey Mare's Tail, Dumfriesshire

NTS reserve, 10 miles NE of Moffat on the A708. Car park and information board showing walks. Guided walks may be available in summer. STOUT FOOTWEAR ESSENTIAL: DANGEROUS TO LEAVE PATHS.

The short path to the left (SW) of the Tail Burn leads to a dramatic 200ft (60m) waterfall, on the rocks beside which grow Goldenrod, Dog's Mercury, Wood Sage and Roseroot. The high path, right of the stream, leads to Loch Skeen (allow at least 2 hours), with Alpine Lady's-mantle and other arctic-alpines amongst the scree beyond the reach of feral goats and Cloudberry on peaty areas.

4. Falls of Clyde, Lanarkshire

SWT reserve. From Lanark follow signs for New Lanark, 1 mile S of town centre. Park in village. Visitor centre signposted beyond mill buildings. Leaflet avalable from centre.

A rough footpath leads through attractive woodland beside the River Clyde to the spectacular Corra Linn waterfall. Woodland flowers include Wood Anemone, Bluebell, Dog's Mercury, Common Cow-wheat, and, more rarely, Northern Bedstraw, Wood Vetch and Common Wintergreen. Marsh Marigold, Cuckooflower, Meadowsweet and Water Avens grow by the river.

Oysterplant grows rarely at Ballantrae, but is slightly more frequent (though never common) on shingly shores further north

231

Goatfell on Arran. Photo by Glyn Satterley

5. Goatfell, Arran

NTS reserve, N of Brodick, approached by paths up Glen Rosa, Glen Sannox or starting in Brodick Country Park along the Cnocan burn. STOUT FOOTWEAR ESSENTIAL.

Heath Milkwort, Heath Spotted-orchid and Sundews grow on the lower reaches of the walk up this dramatic 2,867ft (874m) hill. Mountain Sorrel and Starry Saxifrage grow beside the streams, and Dwarf Willow on the windswept tops.

6. Glen Nant, Argyll

NNR and Caledonian Forest Reserve beside B845 road 4 miles S of Taynuilt. Nature trail and short disabled trail from Forestry Commission car park signed on W of road. STOUT FOOTWEAR ADVISABLE.

This attractive Ash, Hazel, Oak and Birch woodland was once coppiced for charcoal for the Bonawe Furnace (an ancient monument in Taynuilt village). Beneath the lichen-encrusted trees grow Sanicle, Wild Hyacinth, Ramsons, Wood Anemone, Primroses and, much more rarely, Globeflower and Bird's-nest Orchid, while Blaeberry, Bell Heather and Common Cow-wheat grow in the poorer birch woodland.

SOUTH-EAST SCOTLAND

7. Lindean Reservoir, Selkirkshire

About 4 miles E of Selkirk on the A699, turn left (N) onto minor road to Lindean village; reservoir 1 mile on left. Park by information cairn; follow muddy path round reservoir.

This disused reservoir is managed by Borders Regional Council for its wildlife. Plants of wet areas include Greater and Lesser Spearwort, Cuckooflower, Water Avens, Grass-of-Parnassus, Bogbean, Amphibious Bistort, Skullcap and Early and Northern Marsh-orchids. Fairy Flax, Mountain Pansy, Common Rock-rose, Bird's-foot Trefoil and Common Spotted Orchid grow in lime-rich grassland.

8. River Tweed, St Boswells, Roxburghshire

Limited parking where B6404 crosses River Tweed at Mertoun Bridge, SE of St Boswells. Keep to public footpath leading upstream along riverbank to St Boswells (or on to Newton St Boswells). Good parking also in both towns.

This path leads through attractive woodland with Marsh Marigold, Water Avens and Butterbur by the river, and Wood Stitchwort, Meadow Saxifrage, Goldilocks Buttercup, Primrose, Moschatel, Wild Garlic, Few-flowered Leek and Leopardsbane beneath the trees.

9. St Abb's Head NNR, Berwickshire

NTS/SWT reserve. From Coldingham on A1107, take B6438 towards St Abb's. About 3 miles on, car park and nature centre signed on left at Northfield Farm. Guide leaflet available. STOUT FOOTWEAR ESSENTIAL.

A rough footpath leads to spectacular cliffs with nesting seabirds. Primrose, Thrift, Early Purple Orchid and Purple Milk-vetch grow beside the path to the clifftop. Further north, where the path cuts inland past a sheltered grassy bank below Kirk Hill, look for Cowslip, Lady's Bedstraw, Thyme and Common Rock-rose. Kidney Vetch, Spring Sandwort and Common Rock-rose grow on banks by the lighthouse road, and Sea Campion, Roseroot and Scots Lovage are easily visible on inaccessible cliffs.

10. John Muir Country Park, East Lothian

Nature trail starts from car parks at N end of Dunbar High Street or by shore at Belhaven, E of Dunbar. Guide leaflet available from Tourist Information Centres.

This excellent nature trail, with informative display boards, leads along coastal grassland and clifftop. The introduced Hoary Cress (*Cardaria draba*) grows near Belhaven, and other plants include Buckshorn Plantain, Sea Campion, Common Scurvy-grass, Thrift, Meadow Saxifrage, Cowslip and Biting Stonecrop.

11. Yellowcraig, East Lothian

From Dirleton, off the A198 W of North Berwick, follow signs for caravan site to large car park. Sandy track to dunes. Guide leaflet available from car park attendant or Tourist Information Centres.

Yellow Figwort and Spring Beauty grow in the wood before the dunes and Hemlock and Viper's Bugloss in the rough grassland. In the dunes, look for Eyebright, Common Restharrow, Purple Milk-vetch, Spring Vetch, Fairy Flax, Dovesfoot Cranesbill and Rue-leaved Saxifrage, with Grass-of-Parnassus in damp hollows and Scots Lovage amongst the Marram Grass.

Red Campion is one of the commoner plants growing in the dunes at Yellowcraig, with the island of Fidra in the background

Common Rock-rose is a lime-loving plant which flowers in June on the rich rocks on the south side of Holyrood Park

12. Holyrood Park, Edinburgh

Historic Scotland site. Park opposite Duddingston Loch at the SE entrance and climb

steps behind gatehouse to Dunsapie, or park beside Dunsapie Loch on the Queen's
Drive (high road through Park). BEWARE TRAFFIC.

Walk down the road SW from Dunsapie and explore the rocks
on the right of the road for Bloody Cranesbill, Vipers Bugloss,
Spring Sandwort, Common Rock-rose, Garlic Mustard, and
Common and Oxford Ragwort. The rocks beneath Arthur's Seat
(823ft; 251m) have Ling, Bell Heather and Blaeberry, with
Purple Milk-vetch and Burnet Rose in richer soils.

13. Inversnaid, Loch Lomond, Stirlingshire

Approach from B829 NW of Aberfoyle, following minor road W to Inversnaid car
park. Passenger ferries in summer from Inveruglas on the W side of Loch Lomond.

This RSPB reserve is easily explored from the West Highland
Way along 'the bonnie banks' north of Inversnaid. In spring,
there are glorious displays of Bluebell, Wood Sorrel, Ramsons,
Wood Anemone, Lesser Celandine, Primrose, Sanicle and
Woodruff beneath open woodland of Ash, Alder, Oak and Birch.

14. Tentsmuir Point NNR, Fife

From Leuchars, N of St Andrews, follow minor road signed to Kinshaldy car park
(Forestry Commission) and walk towards beach.

The dunes here, clothed in Marram and Lyme Grass, have grown
800yds (730m) seaward in 40 years. Common and Seaside
Centaury, Purple Milk-vetch, Grass-of-Parnassus, Crowberry
and Coralroot Orchid are amongst 400 species recorded.

The view through woods across Loch Lomond towards mountains at
Inversnaid RSPB reserve. Photo CH Gomersall, RSPB

NORTH-EAST SCOTLAND

15. Coire Gabhail, Glencoe

Park in rough car park on S side of road in middle of Pass of Glencoe. Walk E along old road, cross bridge, and follow rocky path up hill. STOUT FOOTWEAR ESSENTIAL.

Although steep, this path is safe with care and the scenery is magnificent. It leads over the sheer lip of the corrie into the hanging ('lost') valley of Coire Gabhail (pronounced 'Corrie Gy-al'). Arctic-alpines on the valley floor include Starry and Yellow Saxifrage, Moss Campion, Alpine Lady's-mantle, Roseroot and Mountain Sorrel.

In the Coire Gabhail, mountain plants such as Yellow Saxifrage (above) grow in a magnificent alpine setting

16. Birks of Aberfeldy, Perthshire

Car park signed off A826 on S outskirts of Aberfeldy. Walk S along woodland track. Guide leaflet available from Tourist Information Centre.

The 3 mile path to the Falls of Moness leads through attractive birch woodland ('birks'), with Bird's-nest Orchid, Wood Vetch, Wood Cranesbill, Chickweed Wintergreen, Common Cow-wheat, Common Wintergreen and Alpine Bistort in places beneath the trees.

*Melancholy Thistle is a
northern species which flowers
abundantly in Brerechen
Meadow in July.
Photo Sue Scott*

17. Brerechan Meadow, Perthshire

*Small SWT reserve on S side of A924 Pitlochry-Blairgowrie road, 1 mile E of
telephone box at Dalnavaid and 3 miles W of Straloch School. Park in layby by small
bridge. VIEW FROM ROAD: NO ACCESS TO MEADOW.*

This narrow strip of flood meadow, sandwiched between river
and road, is full of colour in June and July, with Globeflower,
Marsh Marigold, Wood Cranesbill, Water Avens, Lady's
Bedstraw, Meadowsweet and Melancholy Thistle visible from
the road.

18. Glenshee, Angus/Aberdeenshire

*On the A93 Blairgowrie-Braemar road, park in large car park for Glenshee Ski Area
(15 miles S of Braemar) and explore peaty grassland W of road.*

Common Cow-wheat, Chickweed Wintergreen, Mountain
Pansy and masses of Cloudberry grow on the peat beside the road
(at 2,100ft; 650m). Gravelly streamside flushes support Yellow
and Starry Saxifrage, Scots Asphodel, Alpine Meadow-rue and
Alpine Bistort. Alternatively, take the chairlift to the summit
ridge, where Crowberry and Trailing Azalea grow.

19. St Cyrus NNR, Angus

*From A92 3½ miles N of Montrose, take minor road E along the N bank of the River
N Esk. After about 1½ miles, car park signed on left (W) of road. Cross road and
enter reserve by obvious path into dunes. Guide leaflet available.*

Lady's Bedstraw, Maiden Pink, Clustered Bellflower, Lesser Meadow-rue and Purple Milk-vetch grow amongst the dunes of this attractive reserve (see p. 98), and Wood Vetch, Common Restharrow, Wild Liquorice (*Astragalus glycyphyllos*), Haresfoot Clover, Hemp Agrimony, Marjoram and Carline Thistle are found by the obvious path up the cliff.

Clustered Bellflower (Campanula glomerata)*, resembling Giant Bellflower (p.144) but with long-stalked root leaves and upward-facing, stalkless flowers, grows in the dunes at St Cyrus and a few other lime-rich E coast sites.*

20. Muir of Dinnet NNR, Royal Deeside

Car park and Visitor Centre at Burn O'Vat on the A97, 1 mile NE of junction with the A93 (5 miles E of Ballater). Walk from here along signed Burn O'Vat trail.

This trail illustrates the landforms of the area, with impressive views across the partly birch- and pine-covered moorland. Typical plants of the Muir (moor) along the trail include Heather, Bell Heather, Cross-leaved Heath, Bearberry, Petty Whin, Chickweed Wintergreen and a few plants of Intermediate Wintergreen.

21. Loch Garten, Inverness-shire

RSPB reserve. Follow signs towards osprey hide E of Boat of Garten. About ½ mile W of the hide car park, follow woodland track S to Loch Mallachie.

This looped path leads through attractive pine woodland, beneath which grow Common Cow-wheat, Petty Whin,

Common, Serrated and Chickweed Wintergreen and Creeping
Lady's-tresses Orchid.

22. Spey Bay, Morayshire

*From A96 at Mosstodloch, 1 mile W of Fochabers, take the B9015 to Kingston. Car
park at W end of village and walk along track to W, taking left fork after 270yds
(250m).*

This SWT reserve is part of the largest vegetated shingle beach
in Scotland. Plants by the track include Kidney Vetch, Common
Restharrow, Burnet Rose, Common Wintergreen, Field
Gentian, and Coralroot, Lesser Butterfly and Northern Marsh
Orchids, although care should be taken when searching for the
inconspicuous Coralroot not to damage other vegetation.

NORTH-WEST SCOTLAND

*The yellow-flowered, seaside subspecies of Wild Pansy (subspecies curtisii)
is a common plant in the machair of the Uists*

23. South Uist Machair, Outer Hebrides

*Explore from minor roads W of the A865 around Bornish, Howmore or Kilpheder
(SW of Daliburgh). KEEP OUT OF PLOUGHED CROFT LAND AND BIRD-
NESTING AREAS.*

The machair is full of colour in summer (see p. 19), with Red and
White Clover, Kidney Vetch, Tufted Vetch, Eyebright, Lady's
Bedstraw, Lesser Meadow-rue and Red Bartsia. On the edges of

ploughed areas, look for Corn Marigold, Bugloss, Knotgrass, Common Fumitory, Sun Spurge and Long-headed Poppy.

24. Balranald, North Uist, Outer Hebrides

RSPB reserve. From A865 7 miles N of Clachan-a-Luib, take minor road W signed to Houghary (NOT Balranald). Bear left after 1 mile and park near RSPB sign. Follow track past reception cottage then SW towards Aird an Runair. CROFT LAND SO RESPECT CROFTING ACTIVITIES.

The dune subspecies of Early Marsh Orchid grows near the car park, and the machair beyond has many of the flowers listed for S Uist Machair (above), plus Sea Sandwort, Frog Orchid and the seaside subspecies of Wild Pansy (p. 239). Ragged Robin and Northern Marsh-orchid grow in wetter areas, and Sea Sandwort and Scots Lovage around the sandy bay N of the path.

The slumped landscape of the Storr in Skye produces dramatic cliffs and pinnacles beneath which grow a number of uncommon plants, including the inconspicuous Iceland Purslane, a tiny relative of Docks

25. Old Man of Storr, Skye

Park in layby by A865 at N end of Loch Leathan, 6 miles N of Portree. A footpath, newly restored by the District Council and SNH (opening summer 1995) leads from here through woodland, also being restored, to the Old Man (rock pinnacle). STOUT FOOTWEAR ESSENTIAL.

Amongst breathtaking cliffs and pinnacles, arctic-alpine flowers grow at relatively low altitude, including Globeflower, Northern Rock-cress, Moss Campion, Alpine Lady's-mantle, Purple and Mossy Saxifrages, Mountain Sorrel and Roseroot. Gravel N of the Old Man is home to the rare but inconspicuous Iceland Purslane (*Koenigia islandica*).

The attractive natural pinewood beside Loch Maree at Beinn Eighe. Photo Laurie Campbell

26. Beinn Eighe NNR, Wester Ross

Two waymarked trails from large car park E of A832 beside Loch Maree, 2½ miles NW of Kinlochewe. Guide leaflets available from Visitor Centre (1 mile NW of Kinlochewe).

The signposted Glas Leitire Trail (1 mile) is fairly easy walking. Beneath magnificent Scots Pines, Serrated and Chickweed Wintergreens and Creeping Lady's-tresses Orchid grow amongst the heathers, with Globeflower, Water Avens, Common Wintergreen and Melancholy Thistle in craggy ground higher up the hillside. The steeper Mountain Trail (4 miles; STOUT FOOTWEAR ESSENTIAL) climbs to 1,770ft (540m) and plants to be seen include Dwarf Cornel, Crowberry, Trailing Azalea and Alpine Bearberry.

27. Knockan Cliff, Wester Ross

Part of the Inverpolly NNR. Nature trail starts from Knockan Centre, signposted off A835 15 miles N of Ullapool. Guide leaflet available from Centre.

The Knockan Trail displays spectacular scenery and a fine range of flowers on the limestone cliffs, including Alpine Bistort, Alpine Lady's-mantle, Crowberry, Yellow Saxifrage, Opposite-leaved Golden-saxifrage, Mountain Avens, Stone Bramble and Autumn Gentian.

28. Durness, Sutherland

Park at Balnakeil on NW outskirts of Durness village and walk to Faraid Head.

Mountain Avens grows abundantly in limestone grassland here, along with Alpine Bistort, Yellow Saxifrage and Hoary Whitlow-grass. Scots Primrose is common in low grassland where shell sand and salt spray blow inland, W of Balnakeil, and Roseroot and Wild Angelica grow on the cliffs of Faraid Head.

The low grassland behind this Spear Thistle at Durness is the home of Scots Primrose. Photo Sue Scott

29. Invernaver NNR, Sutherland

About 5 miles W of Bettyhill on A836 take minor road N through Borgie, 3 miles beyond, park at roadside at SW corner of Torrisdale Bay. Cross footbridge and follow obvious path over hill to cliff and dunes beside mouth of R. Naver.

Where windblown sand enriches the cliff grassland – and in the sandy shingle below – a fine range of arctic-alpine and lime-loving flowers grows, including Moss Campion, Purple Oxytropis, Kidney Vetch, Fairy Flax, Mountain Avens, Yellow and Purple Saxifrages, Autumn Gentian, Small-white Orchid and Dark-red Helleborine.

30. Dunnet Head, Caithness

Follow B855 N from Dunnet (9 miles E of Thurso) to car park before lighthouse. PRIVATE OPEN LAND SO RESPECT LANDOWNER'S INTERESTS.

Scots Primrose and Spring Squill grow in windswept turf on the clifftop, while the cliffs support Roseroot, Scots Lovage and Alpine Saw-wort (*Saussurea alpina*). On moorland areas just inland, Crowberry, Bearberry, Alpine Bearberry and Dwarf Willow can be found.

NORTHERN ISLES

31. Old Man of Hoy, Orkney

RSPB reserve. Car ferry to Hoy from Houton, SE of Stromness. From ferry terminal, follow B9047 N for 8 miles then turn left onto minor road to Rackwick. Car park signed at road end.

The road past the Youth Hostel leads to a peaty track to the Old Man, a 450ft (137m) rock stack. Bearberry, Alpine Bearberry, Mountain Everlasting and Heath Spotted Orchid grow by the path, and Red and Sea Campion, Primrose, Spring Squill and Roseroot on the cliffs overlooking the Old Man.

Thrift, Roseroot, Bird's-foot Trefoil and Sea Campion hang onto the cliffs near the Old Man of Hoy beside nesting Fulmars

32. Yesnaby, Mainland, Orkney

5 miles N of Stromness on B905, take minor road W, signed to Yesnaby. Park near ruins at road end and walk S over cliff grassland. PRIVATE OPEN LAND SO RESPECT LANDOWNER'S INTERESTS.

This is one of the best known sites for Scots Primrose, which grows in grassy heathland with Mountain Everlasting, Thrift, Bird's-foot Trefoil, Grass-of-Parnassus, Spring Squill and Devil's-bit Scabious.

33. North Hill, Papa Westray, Orkney

RSPB reserve. Car ferry to Papa Westray from Kirkwall. Walk along road to N end of island. Reserve entrance signposted. CROFT LAND SO RESPECT CROFTING ACTIVITIES. Summer warden can advise on plant sites. Excellent hostel on island.

The grassy heathland here has localised patches of Mountain Everlasting, Grass-of-Parnassus, Scots Primrose and Alpine Meadow-rue. Thrift, Sea Campion, and Sea Milkwort grow on the rocks, and Sea Rocket and Sea Sandwort in the North Wick dunes.

Scots Primrose, a species only found in Caithness, Sutherland and Orkney, grows in the windswept, clifftop grasslands of Yesnaby and the North Hill of Papa Westray

The deep-red flowers of Shetland Red Campion (subspecies zetlandica) grow in many wet meadows and roadside verges around the islands

34. Mousa Island, Shetland

Ferry from Sand Lodge, signed off the A970 12 miles S of Lerwick; book with boatman, Tom Jamieson (tel: Sandwick 367).

Sea Campion, Thrift, Scots Lovage and Danish Scurvy-grass grow on low cliffs between the ferry landing and the famous 1st Century BC Broch tower (an Ancient Monument). Cross the island E of the Broch, avoiding the terns, to the seal-inhabited West Pool, beside which grow Sea Milkwort, Sea Sandwort, Sea Arrowgrass, Sea Plantain, Curved Sedge (*Carex maritima*) and Moss Campion at unusually low altitude, with Chickweed Wintergreen in grassland at the N of the island.

35. Ronas Hill, North Mainland, Shetland

Access on foot from private road up Collafirth Hill W of A970 12½ miles N of Brae, then walk towards summit. STOUT FOOTWEAR ESSENTIAL.

Crowberry, Bilberry, Bog Bilberry, Bell Heather, Trailing Azalea, Alpine Bistort, Dwarf Willow, Sea Plantain, Mountain Everlasting and Slender St.John's-wort grow in the mossy patches on this windswept, arctic boulder-field, terraced by frost movement and rising to a summit of 1,475ft (450m).

36. Keen of Hamar NNR, Unst, Shetland

Inter-island ferry to Unst via Yell. Follow A968 N through Baltasound village. Where main road bends N, carry straight on (E) to Little Hamar. Park carefully at roadside and walk N along fence-line entering reserve at gate by display board.

The serpentine rock of this low hill (289ft; 88m) is toxic to much plant growth, producing a bare, rocky landscape. The plants in the serpentine debris are few but remarkable, including Alpine Meadow-rue, Northern Rock-cress (*Cardaminopsis petraea*), Shetland Mouse-ear (*Cerastium nigrescens*), Hoary Whitlow-grass (*Draba incana*), Norwegian Sandwort (*Arenaria norvegica*), Kidney Vetch, Stone Bramble, Sea Plantain, Mountain Everlasting and Frog Orchid.

Shetland Mouse-ear is found in the serpentine gravel around the Keen of Hamar, and nowhere else in the world

FURTHER INFORMATION: A number of excellent local Floras (annotated flower lists) are now available for many parts of Scotland and are well worth seeking out in local bookshops. Information from several of these has been drawn on in compiling the species accounts in this book.

CONSERVING SCOTLAND'S FLORA

Unless plant-rich meadows can be protected, plants like Globeflower will continue to become rarer

In Scotland, as elsewhere, many pressures affect the native flora. Some are localised effects, caused by the demands of human development; others are more insidious, worldwide problems resulting from pollution and climate change. Yet Scotland retains a rich variety of plant life.

There are two main explanations for this. Firstly, the population density of Scotland (65 people per square kilometre, dropping to 8 per square kilometre in the Highlands) is low. As a result, the pressure on land is reduced, allowing flower-rich corners to survive. Secondly, 95 per cent of Scotland is described, in farming terms, as a 'Less Favoured Area' (a very arguable term!). This results from a combination of climate and soil which makes intensive agriculture uneconomic and triggers European subsidies supporting lower-intensity agriculture. Consequently, less land is ploughed and fewer farm chemicals are used, allowing more wild flowers to survive.

But, inevitably, there are pressures on flower-rich sites, especially in the lowlands, as towns expand and development is targeted in the countryside. Agriculture and forestry continue to erode wild corners, constrained only slightly by the European system of farm 'set-aside' and more sympathetic grant conditions.

Meadows and wetlands have been particularly badly affected by farming and other development, and lowland peat bogs are threatened by the continuing extraction of peat for horticulture, despite the wide availability of peat-free alternatives. Conservation bodies like the Scottish Wildlife Trust (SWT) and Plantlife are campaigning against the destruction of these important flower habitats, and the SWT has acquired a number of meadows, bogs and wetlands as nature reserves.

In many upland areas, heavy sheep grazing reduces the variety of wild flowers. Even more seriously, the high population of Red Deer – supported by Highland estates for the sport of deer stalking – is seriously damaging plant communities and is the main cause of the decline of native pinewoods. Although Red Deer have an important place in Highland ecology, their population

Unnaturally large numbers of Red Deer in many parts of the Highlands are stopping native pinewoods from regenerating

will need to be greatly reduced if they are to live in balance with their environment.

The government conservation agency, Scottish

Natural Heritage (SNH), and the Forestry Commission are now making considerable efforts to restore native woodlands. SNH also has responsibility for protecting the key nature conservation sites in Scotland, notified as Sites of Special Scientific Interest (SSSIs), some of which are also being designated as Special Areas for Conservation under European Union directives. Although most of these are privately-owned, SNH has some ability to encourage sound management by grants to the land owners.

Some larger areas are also designated as National Nature Reserves, and here SNH has a more active role in managing the nature conservation interest, although, uniquely in Europe, few of these sites are state-owned. As a result, the landowner's legitimate interests sometimes restrict nature conservation management. Scotland has no National Parks.

To ensure positive, long-term management, voluntary conservation bodies including the SWT, Royal Society for the Protection of Birds, National Trust for Scotland, Woodland Trust and John Muir Trust have bought large tracts of land where nature conservation becomes the prime objective. These bodies, which rely on public support for their work, have a key role in protecting the wild flowers that are such an integral part of Scotland's landscape.

Dark-red Helleborine (Epipactis atrorubens) is a handsome orchid found in a few limestone areas in north-west Scotland, several of which are protected as nature reserves or SSSIs

INDEX

In the index of common names below, a reference to 'species' (as in 'Arrowgrass species') means that more than one related species is featured on that page/spread. Page references in **bold** refer to main species entries and in *italics* to photographs. This is followed by a scientific index, arranged by genus to aid comparisons between related species.

INDEX